The Hou

Adaptation by **Jeremy Fitzgerald**
Activities by **Louis Vaughan**
Illustrated by **Didi Coppola**

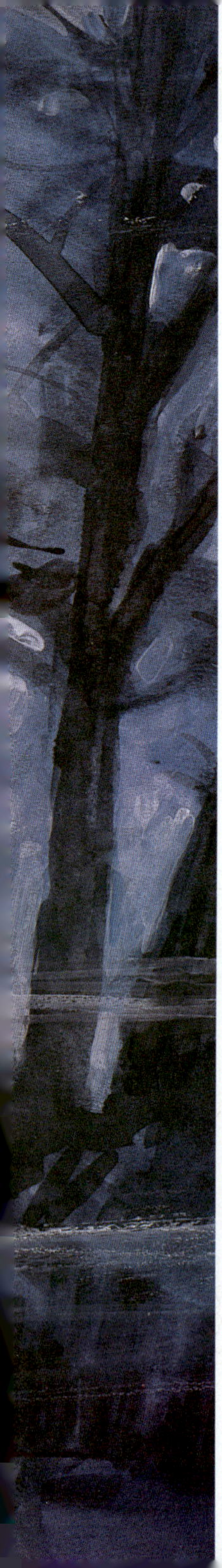

Editors: Emma Berridge, Frances Evans
Design and art direction: Nadia Maestri
Computer graphics: Simona Corniola
Illustrations: Didi Coppola
Picture research: Laura Lagomarsino

First edition, 2004
First reprint, 2008
Second reprint, 2011
Third reprint, 2014

Legal Deposit: B. 21.352-2011
ISBN: 978-84-316-7820-3
V.V. Order Nº: GM34

PRINTED IN SPAIN.

Contents

PET Cambridge **P**reliminary **E**nglish **T**est-style exercises

T: GRADE 6 Trinity-style exercises (Grade 6)

This story is recorded in full.

END These symbols indicate the chapters and exercises featured on the accompanying CD.

Sir Arthur Conan Doyle (1927) by Henry L. Gates.

Sir Arthur *Conan Doyle* (1859-1930)

Today most people know Sir Arthur Conan Doyle as the creator of one of the best-known fictional characters in the world, Sherlock Holmes. But Conan Doyle was also one of the most remarkable personalities of his time.

Conan Doyle was born in 1859 in Edinburgh. His mother, Mary Foley, inspired her son's passion for literature. His father, Charles Doyle, came from an artistic family, but suffered from alcoholism and epilepsy.

When Conan Doyle was 17, his father was sent to a mental hospital. Perhaps Conan Doyle decided to study medicine at Edinburgh University and not follow his artistic interests because of this sad event.

At Edinburgh University he also worked for Dr Joseph Bell. Dr Bell amazed[1] his students with his ability to guess many things about his patients by just looking at them. Dr Bell later became the model for Sherlock Holmes.

After graduating,[2] Conan Doyle set up a medical practice.[3] He had few patients so he had a lot of time to write. One of the stories he wrote was *A Study in Scarlet*. This was the first Sherlock Holmes story.

From the beginning Conan Doyle wrote the Sherlock Holmes stories to make money. His real passion was writing historical novels, and his historical novel *Micah Clarke* (1889) was a big success.

In 1891, a monthly magazine, the *Strand*, commissioned him to write six Sherlock Holmes stories. This magazine had a circulation of 500,000. Further commissions for additional stories followed and Holmes's popularity rapidly grew.

However, Conan Doyle was thinking of 'killing' Holmes because he took time away from his historic novels. So, in 1893, in the story 'The Final Problem', Holmes dies. Conan Doyle's readers were horrified, and 20,000 people cancelled their subscription to the *Strand*.

In 1901, Conan Doyle was finally convinced to bring Holmes back to life. Three collections of stories followed, along with two novels, one of which is *The Hound of the Baskervilles* (1902).

1. **amazed** : greatly surprised.
2. **graduating** : finishing university.
3. **practice** : (here) place where a doctor works.

During the last years of his life, Conan Doyle devoted most of his time and energy to Spiritualism. [1] He went on tours in Europe, America, Australia and Africa to talk about and promote Spiritualism. In 1922, Conan Doyle even declared publicly that he believed in fairies. [2]

After one of these lecture tours in 1929, Conan Doyle returned home exhausted. He then had a heart attack and was ill for several months. He died at his home on 7th July 1930.

1 **Answer the following questions**

- **a.** Who inspired Conan Doyle's passion for literature? Mom
- **b.** What were his father's medical problems? alcolohic and epilepsy
- **c.** How did Dr Bell amaze his students? looking
- **d.** Why did Conan Doyle write Sherlock Holmes stories? Had time
- **e.** Why did Conan Doyle want to 'kill' Sherlock Holmes? took time
- **f.** How did readers of the *Strand* react when Conan Doyle killed Holmes? 20 thousand people canceled subscription
- **g.** What was Conan Doyle's main interest during the last years of his life? Spiritualism

1. **Spiritualism** : belief that it is possible to communicate with the spirits of the dead.
2. **fairies** : 

Characters

Sherlock Holmes

Dr Watson

Henry Baskerville

Mrs Stapleton

Mr Stapleton

Laura Lyons

Mrs Barrymore

Mr Barrymore

Dr Mortimer

CHAPTER **ONE**

The Legend of the Hound [1] of the Baskervilles

One morning, Sherlock Holmes and I were in his flat [2] at 221B Baker Street in London. He was smoking his pipe while we waited for a visitor to arrive. The visitor had come to see us the previous evening, but we had not been there.

Suddenly we heard the doorbell ring: our visitor was here.

'Good morning, Mr Holmes,' the visitor said politely. 'I am Dr Mortimer.' They shook hands.

'This is my friend Dr Watson,' Sherlock Holmes explained. 'He often helps me with my cases.'

'I'm pleased to meet you, Sir,' Dr Mortimer said.

1. **hound** : large dog used for hunting.
2. **flat** : apartment.

Dr Mortimer was a tall man and he was thin. His clothes were smart [1] and he wore glasses. He was a young man but looked older because he was worried.

'I need your advice, Mr Holmes,' he said very seriously.

'Tell us all about it,' Sherlock Holmes said kindly. 'We'll help you if we can.'

Dr Mortimer took some papers out of his pocket.

'A man named Sir Charles Baskerville died about three months ago,' he began. 'He died in a horrible way, as perhaps you know from the newspapers. Before he died he gave me these papers. They tell the story of the Baskerville family. I want to read them to you, if I may?'

'Please go ahead,' Sherlock Holmes agreed. 'We'll listen carefully.'

Dr Mortimer put the papers in front of him and began to read:

I am Hugo Baskerville, and I am writing this in the year 1742. My father told me about the Hound of the Baskervilles, and I believe what he told me. I want you, my sons, to read these words. Remember that God punishes the wicked [2] and forgives the innocent.

The head of the Baskerville family in 1640 was a cruel and bad man. His name was Sir Hugo Baskerville. Sir Hugo fell in love with the daughter of a farmer. She was frightened of him. She always tried to avoid [3] him. One day Sir Hugo learnt that her family were away from the farm.

1. **smart** : elegant.
2. **wicked** : evil, extremely bad.
3. **avoid** : stay away from.

He rode [1] to the farm with some friends of his and they carried the girl to Baskerville Hall. They locked her in a room upstairs. Then they went downstairs and started to eat and drink. The girl was terrified. She jumped out of the window and tried to run back to her home.

Sir Hugo was furious when he realised her room was empty. He was also very drunk by now. His friends told him to let out the hounds and he agreed to do this. Then he jumped on his horse and rode after the hounds.

Some of his friends also decided to ride after him.

After a while Sir Hugo's friends saw an old man in the darkness. They wanted to know where Sir Hugo was. The old man seemed very frightened and could hardly [2] speak.

'I saw Sir Hugo on his horse,' the old man told them. 'But I also saw a huge hound. It was running silently beside Sir Hugo.'

Sir Hugo's friends laughed at the old man's words, but their laughter did not last long. Soon they saw Sir Hugo's horse. It was coming towards them, but it was alone.

The men now rode deeper into the moor [3] in order to find their friend. They found the hounds at the edge of a deep valley. Baskerville hounds are usually very courageous, but these ones seemed terrified. They did not want to go further into the valley.

1. **rode** : (ride, rode, ridden) travelled by horse.
2. **hardly** : only just.
3. **moor** : wide open area covered with short grass.

A few of Sir Hugo's friends went into the valley. They saw two great stones on the ground there. The farmer's daughter lay near one of these stones — she was dead. Sir Hugo was on the ground next to her. The men were frightened now, because there was an enormous hound standing over Sir Hugo. The hound moved forward and tore out[1] *Sir Hugo's throat.*[2] *Then it turned slowly towards the men. It was the biggest hound they had ever seen. Its eyes and body shone*[3] *in the darkness.*

The men galloped away. One of them died of fright when they reached Baskerville Hall. The other two went mad because of what they had seen that night.

That was the first time that the hound appeared. Other Baskervilles have died in strange ways because of that hound. That is why you, my sons, must never cross the moors at night.

Dr Mortimer stopped reading and looked at Sherlock Holmes.

'What do you think?' Dr Mortimer asked anxiously.

'It's a good story to frighten children,' Sherlock Holmes replied.

'There's more,' Dr Mortimer told him.

He took a newspaper article out of his pocket and began to read to us again.

1. **tore out** : (tear, tore, torn) removed with great violence.
2. **throat** : 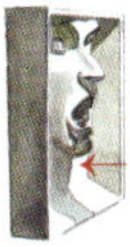
3. **shone** : (shine, shone, shone) gave out light.

Sir Charles Baskerville died very suddenly. He spent only two years at Baskerville because he lived most of his life abroad. He was a good man and he behaved very generously to the poor. We will all miss him.

People are saying strange things about Sir Charles's death. These strange things are not true. Sir Charles died because he had a weak heart. Dr Mortimer says that his heart had been weak for a long time.

The facts of the death are simple. Every evening Sir Charles walked in the gardens around the house. His favourite walk was along the Yew Alley [1] near the house. He went there, as usual, on the evening of the 4th of June to smoke a cigar.

His butler, [2] Barrymore, was upstairs in Sir Charles's room. Sir Charles wanted to go to London the next day. When Sir Charles did not come back to the house Barrymore went into the garden to look for him. He followed his master's footprints [3] in the wet earth. They went from the house, along the Yew Alley, to a gate which opens onto the moors. The footprints stopped at the gate. Barrymore found Sir Charles's body near there.

Barrymore said that his master's footprints were complete until he reached the gate. Then they were not complete. Barrymore thought that Sir Charles was walking on his toes.

The new head of the Baskerville family is Sir Henry Baskerville. He is living in America at present, but the lawyers [4] hope that he will come back to England when he hears the news.

1. **Yew Alley** : long path with yew trees at the side of it.
2. **butler** : male servant.
3. **footprints** : marks left on the ground by the feet.
4. **lawyers** : people who give advice about legal questions.

Go back to the text

PET **1** **For each question, mark the letter next to the correct answer — A, B, C or D.**

1 Where did Dr Mortimer get Hugo Baskerville's papers?
- **A** ☐ Hugo Baskerville gave them to him before he died.
- **B** ☐ Sir Charles Baskerville gave them to him before he died.
- **C** ☐ Hugo Baskerville's sons gave them to him.
- **D** ☐ Sir Henry Baskerville gave them to him.

2 Sir Hugo carried away the daughter of the farmer because
- **A** ☐ he wanted her to work for him.
- **B** ☐ he wanted to frighten her father.
- **C** ☐ he was in love with her.
- **D** ☐ his friend was in love with her.

3 The old man on the moors was very frightened because
- **A** ☐ he knew Sir Hugo was very cruel and wicked.
- **B** ☐ he saw a giant hound running next to Sir Hugo.
- **C** ☐ he saw Sir Hugo's drunken friends.
- **D** ☐ he saw the hounds running after the girl.

4 Sir Hugo's friends began to believe what the old man said when
- **A** ☐ they saw Sir Hugo's horse without Sir Hugo on it.
- **B** ☐ they arrived at the edge of a deep valley.
- **C** ☐ they saw the girl lying on the ground.
- **D** ☐ they saw the hound tear out Sir Hugo's throat.

5 Sir Hugo Baskerville wrote to his sons to tell them
- **A** ☐ a good story.
- **B** ☐ something about local history.
- **C** ☐ why they should not kidnap farm girls.
- **D** ☐ why they should not walk across the moors at night.

6 According to the newspaper article Sir Charles died because
- **A** ☐ he had a weak heart.
- **B** ☐ he had walked out on the moor late at night.
- **C** ☐ he was a wicked man.
- **D** ☐ he smoked too many cigars.

'The men now rode deeper into the moor in order to find their friend'

The **infinitive with 'to'** can be used to show purpose.

- *He called Sarah* ***to wish*** *her a merry Christmas.* =
  He called Sarah because he wanted to wish her a merry Christmas.
- *He bought a newspaper* ***to discover*** *how Sir Charles died.* = He bought the newspaper because he wanted to discover how Sir Charles died.

It is also possible to use **'in order to' with the infinitive.**

- *He called Sarah* ***in order to wish*** *her a merry Christmas.*
- *The men now rode deeper into the moor* ***in order to find*** *their friend.*

2 Complete the following sentences with *in order to* and one of the infinitives from the box, like the example.

avoid	read	take	find	smoke	escape	ask

a. Dr Mortimer came to 221B Baker Street ...in order to ask... Holmes for some advice.

b. Dr Mortimer pulled the papers out of his pocket ...in order to read... them to Holmes.

c. The daughter of the farmer jumped out of the window in order to escape... from Sir Hugo.

d. Sir Hugo went to the girl's farm when her family were away in order to take... her away.

e. Sir Hugo rode out into the moor in order to find the girl.

f. The Baskervilles never cross the moors at night in order to avod... the huge hound.

g. Sir Charles took a walk along the Yew Alley in order to smoke a cigar.

PET **3 Pretend that you live near Baskerville Hall. You have read the article in the newspaper about Sir Charles's death, but you do not agree: you think that the strange things people are saying about Sir Charles's death are true. Write a short letter of about 100 words to the newspaper saying how you think Sir Charles died. You can begin like this.**

Dear Sir,

Like everyone who knew Sir Charles, I am deeply sad about his death. Still, I must say that I do not agree with the newspaper which says

....

Before you read

PET 1 Listen to Chapter Two.
Choose the correct picture and put a tick (✓) in the box below it.

3

1 What kind of animal did Dr Mortimer think he saw among the trees?

A ☐ B ☐ C ☐

2 How high is the Yew hedge?

A ☐ B ☐ C ☐

3 When is Holmes going to meet Sir Henry?

A ☐ B ☐ C ☐

4 What did Holmes do to help him prepare to think?

A ☐ B ☐ C ☐

CHAPTER **TWO**

The Death of Sir Charles Baskerville

'The newspaper tells the story like that,' Dr Mortimer explained to us.

'I read it at the time,' Sherlock Holmes admitted. 'Now I want you to tell us what really happened, Dr Mortimer. Tell us everything that the newspaper did not say.'

'I'm a man of science,' Dr Mortimer said, 'and there are certain things I cannot believe. Besides, I did not want to tell a story that would frighten the new heir [1] to Baskerville Hall. That is why I said nothing to the newspaper reporters. But I will tell you everything, Mr Holmes.'

'Sir Charles was very frightened about something. He believed the stories about the Hound of the Baskervilles. He always asked

1. **heir** : person who owns a property when someone dies.

me questions about it. He said that he heard strange noises at night. He never went out of the house when it was dark, except to walk a little way along the Yew Alley. One night, about three weeks before he died, I found him standing outside the house. He was shaking with terror. [1] He said there was an animal among the trees. I looked and saw an animal there. I thought it was a small cow. I tried to find it but it disappeared. When I came back to the Hall Sir Charles was still very anxious. I stayed with him that night. It was then that he gave me the papers about the family history.'

'Barrymore found Sir Charles's body. He said that the only footprints near Sir Charles's body were Sir Charles's, but he was wrong. I found some other footprints near the body.'

'A man or a woman?' Sherlock Holmes asked excitedly.

'A hound,' the doctor replied quietly, 'a large hound. They were quite clear.' [2]

Sherlock Holmes was very attentive now.

'No one else saw the hound footprints,' he commented. 'Why was that, do you think?'

'The hound prints were not very close to Sir Charles's body,' Dr Mortimer explained. 'I was the only person who examined the area carefully.'

'What about a sheep dog?' asked Sherlock Holmes.

'Sheep dogs do not have such big prints,' the doctor told him.

'And the prints were not very close to the body?' asked Sherlock Holmes.

'No, they were about twenty yards from Sir Charles.'

'Tell me about the Yew Alley,' Sherlock Holmes said to the doctor.

1. **shaking with terror** : moving from side to side in fear.
2. **quite clear** : easily visible.

'There are two yew hedges,' [1] Dr Mortimer explained. 'The hedges are about nine feet [2] high. There is a path between the two hedges. The path has grass at the sides, and there is gravel [3] in the middle.'

'And the gate? Where is the gate?'

'The gate is in one of the hedges,' the doctor told him.

'Is it possible to reach the moor by any other way?' Sherlock Holmes wanted to know.

'No, you have to go through the gate to reach the moors.'

'I see,' said Sherlock Holmes thoughtfully. 'Then you can only enter Yew Alley through the house or through the gate. Is that right?'

'No,' the doctor corrected him. 'There is a summerhouse [4] at the end of the Alley. You can leave the Alley that way.'

'Did Sir Charles reach the summerhouse, Dr Mortimer?'

'We found his body about fifty yards [5] away from the summerhouse,' the doctor confirmed.

'And now the footprints,' Sherlock Holmes said. 'You say that these were on the path, and not on the grass. Is that right?'

'That's right. They were on the same side of the path as the gate that opens onto the moor.'

'Very interesting,' Sherlock Holmes said softly. 'What about the gate itself? Was it open or closed?'

'It was closed and locked,' Dr Mortimer informed him.

1. **hedges** : 
2. **nine feet** : about 3 metres.
3. **gravel** : very small stones used to make paths.
4. **summerhouse** : small construction in a garden, made of wood or glass.
5. **fifty yards** : about 46 metres.

'Is it a tall gate?' Sherlock Holmes wanted to know.

'No,' said the doctor. 'A man could easily jump over it.'

'Tell me more about Sir Charles's footprints, please.'

'I think Sir Charles stood near the gate for some time,' Dr Mortimer said. 'His footprints were everywhere there. There was also cigar ash [1] near the gate.'

'You're a good observer!' Sherlock Holmes complimented him pleasantly. 'But why didn't you come and talk to me at once?' he asked.

The doctor was embarrassed for a moment.

'People are saying strange things,' he began. 'Several people say they have seen a huge animal on the moor. They say it is very large and that it has a strange light. These are sensible, ordinary people, Mr Holmes. I believe they are telling the truth. I didn't know what to do!'

'But you're a man of science!' Sherlock Holmes cried. 'You can't believe in these supernatural stories, surely?'

'I don't know what I believe,' the doctor admitted quietly. 'All I know is this. The hound that killed Sir Hugo in 1640 was a supernatural beast.'

'If you think Sir Charles died because of a supernatural beast, then a detective certainly can't help you!' Holmes said acidly. [2]

'Perhaps you can't,' Dr Mortimer replied. 'But you can give me some advice, Mr Holmes. Sir Henry Baskerville arrives in London today. I want to protect him.'

'Why can't he go to Baskerville Hall?' asked Holmes.

'It's too dangerous for the Baskervilles to be at the Hall!' Dr Mortimer cried desperately.

1. **ash** : burnt material from a cigar or cigarette.
2. **acidly** : sarcastically.

'Very well,' Holmes told him. 'Go and meet Sir Henry. Bring him to me here tomorrow morning at ten o'clock.'

Mortimer left the flat.

***

Holmes and I spent the day apart. When we met later, he asked me a couple of questions about the case.

'Why do you think Sir Charles's footprints changed in the Yew Alley, Watson? Dr Mortimer said they were complete at the beginning of the Alley but he could only see the toes at the end.'

'What do you think, Holmes?' I replied.

'Sir Charles did not walk down the Alley on his toes,' Holmes said decisively. 'He ran. He was frightened. He ran away from something. That's why Dr Mortimer only saw the toe-prints on the path.'

He was silent for a moment.

'There's another question,' he went on. 'Sir Charles was near the gate in the Yew Alley. Why did he wait there? Who was he waiting for, I wonder?'

I looked at my friend Holmes. He seemed pleased. He was always pleased when a case was difficult. He enjoyed thinking. Now he lit his pipe and prepared to think out the problem of the Hound of the Baskervilles.

Go back to the text

PET **1** **Decide if each statement is correct or incorrect. If it is correct, mark A. If it is not correct, mark B.**

T F
A B

1 Sir Charles believed that there was a huge, supernatural dog on the moors.
2 Sir Charles often went out at night to walk across the moors.
3 Barrymore found a woman's footprints near Sir Charles body.
4 There are three entrances to the Yew Alley.
5 Dr Mortimer thinks that Sir Charles walked to the gate and then left it immediately.
6 Dr Mortimer believes the stories about the huge hound on the moors.
7 Sir Charles walked on his toes to get away from something that frightened him.

Now correct the incorrect statements.

2 **But you're a man of science!**

a. Complete this table about the hound.

The hound in legend	
When it was first seen	1640
What it did when it was first seen	kill sir hugo
The hound today	Sir Charles and Mortimer
Who has seen or heard it	~~Several peopple~~ Super Natural
How it is described	larg and stnge light
Role in the death of Sir Charles	The killer

b. What do you think? Does any of the information you have collected about the hound make you think it really exits?

'But you can give me some advice'

Countable nouns are nouns that we can make plural and can count.

A horse — Two horses

A table — Three tables

Uncountable nouns cannot be made plural and are not used with ***a*** or ***an***.

- The names of substances are usually uncountable in English. For example, *milk, coffee, wood, bread, toothpaste, soap* and *ice.*
- There are also many uncountable nouns in English that are not always uncountable in other languages. For example:

  Work is uncountable but *job* is countable:

  - *Courtney is looking for work.* (Uncountable)
  - *Courtney is looking for a job.* (Countable)

  Uncountable nouns can be preceded by *a lot of, a bit of, no, some* and *any.*

  I don't have any luggage.

  She has no information about the trains to Amsterdam.

3 **Fill in the gaps with a suitable uncountable noun from the box.**

~~rubbish~~	~~advice~~	~~news~~	~~progress~~	information	~~traffic~~	~~hair~~

a. Karen: How's your Chinese class going?
Donna: Well, I am making some ...progress... . Now, I can understand simple conversations.

b. Peter: Have you heard the ...news... about Jamie?
Jane: No, I haven't.
Peter: She is marrying a man from Dundee.

c. Let me give you some ...advice... about our boss. Never argue with him.

d. I looked on the Internet for some ...information... about whales.

e. Karim: Why is there ...rubbish... in front of the house?
Nicole: The neighbours had a party last night, and they haven't cleaned up yet.

f. My girlfriend has short, red ...hair... .

g. When there is not a lot of ...traffic..., I can drive to work in less than twenty minutes.

PET **4** Sherlock Holmes now has a lot of information about this case. Talk together with a partner about some things he may need to help him solve the mystery. Decide which are the most important. (Use your dictionary to help you.)
Here is a picture with some ideas to help you.

Before you read

PET 1 **Listen to the beginning of Chapter Three. For each question, put a tick (✓) in the correct box.**

4

1 What time did Dr Mortimer and Sir Henry Baskerville arrive at Holmes's flat?

A ☐ eleven o'clock
B ☐ nine o'clock
C ☐ ten o'clock

2 What was Sir Henry like?

A ☐ He was a tall, strong-looking man.
B ☐ He was a small, strong-looking man.
C ☐ He was a small, weak-looking man.

3 The letter said that Sir Henry's life was in danger

A ☐ in London.
B ☐ on the moors.
C ☐ in America.

4 What did Sir Henry lose in the hotel?

A ☐ a shoe
B ☐ his wallet
C ☐ some luggage

5 The passenger in the taxi had

A ☐ a black beard.
B ☐ a red beard.
C ☐ a large black moustache.

CHAPTER **THREE**

A Mysterious Man in a London Taxi

Dr Mortimer and Sir Henry Baskerville arrived at the flat at ten o'clock the next morning. Sir Henry was a small, strong-looking man.

'I'm happy Mortimer arranged this meeting,' he told Sherlock Holmes. 'I received this letter this morning.'

He handed the letter to Sherlock Holmes who read it aloud.

'Don't go to the moor. Your life is in danger.'

'What does it mean?' Sir Henry asked Holmes.

'Have you anything else to tell me?' Sherlock Holmes asked him.

'Not really,' Sir Henry replied. 'But something strange happened at my hotel last night. I left my shoes outside the room for the boots [1] to clean them. When I woke up this morning there was only one shoe outside the room. It's annoying because the shoes are new. I've never worn them.'

Sherlock Holmes then explained the Baskerville family story to Sir Henry.

'Now we need to decide whether it is too dangerous for you to go to Baskerville Hall,' he said.

'Baskerville Hall is my family house!' Sir Henry replied angrily. 'No one will stop me from going there if I want to. Why don't you

1. **boots** : (here) hotel servant who cleans guests's shoes.

join me for lunch in two hours at my hotel and we can discuss the whole matter?'[1]

Dr Mortimer and Sir Henry walked out of the flat.

'Quick, Watson!' Sherlock Holmes cried. 'I want to follow them. Sir Henry may be in danger.'

We followed the two men without difficulty. Suddenly Holmes touched my arm. He pointed to a taxi that was going along the road near the doctor and Sir Henry. There was a passenger in the taxi – a man with a black beard.

END

1. **matter** : subject, case.

The passenger saw us and ordered the driver to move away quickly.

'It's not important,' Holmes told me. 'I took the driver's number. I'll talk to him later.'

When we arrived at Sir Henry's hotel Sir Henry told us that someone had taken another of his shoes – this time one of an old pair. Holmes seemed interested in this piece of news but he did not say anything.

Sir Henry told us that he was going to Baskerville Hall.

'You're doing the right thing,' Holmes encouraged him. 'If someone is trying to hurt you, you're safer there than in London.'

Then Holmes described the passenger in the taxi.

'Is there anyone at Baskerville Hall who has a black beard?' he asked Dr Mortimer.

'Only Barrymore, the butler,' Dr Mortimer replied.

'Good,' said Holmes. 'I'll send a telegram to the house to ask Barrymore if everything is ready for the arrival of Sir Henry. I'll instruct the post office to give Barrymore his telegram personally. Then we'll know if the butler is in London or at Baskerville Hall today!'

Then Holmes asked about the money that came to different people after the death of Sir Charles.

'Barrymore and his wife received £500, and I received £1,000,' the doctor explained. 'The rest goes to Sir Henry – about £740,000.'

'It's a lot of money,' Holmes said thoughtfully. 'Some people would kill for a fortune like that. What happens if Sir Henry dies? Where does the money go then?'

Mortimer gave a long explanation of the members of the Baskerville family.

'Sir Charles had two brothers. Sir Henry is the only son of Sir Charles's second brother. The third brother, Rodger, was a criminal. He ran away to South America in order to avoid the police in England. He died in South America. Therefore, if Sir Henry dies, everything goes to a cousin, James Desmond. James Desmond is an old man. He does not want to be rich.'

Now Sherlock Holmes gave Sir Henry some advice.

'Go to Baskerville Hall tomorrow,' he said, 'but do not go there alone. I can't come with you at the moment because I'm working on another case, but take Watson with you.'

Sir Henry and I were happy with Holmes's suggestion.

'Look!' cried Sir Henry suddenly. 'This is one of the shoes that I couldn't find before. It was under the table.'

'It wasn't there when we searched this room,' Dr Mortimer commented in surprise.

Holmes and I returned to the Baker Street flat.

There was a knock on the door. It was the taxi driver who had driven the passenger with the black beard.

'What can I do for you, Sir?' the man asked Holmes politely.

'Tell me about the passenger you had today,' Holmes told him. 'The passenger with the black beard.'

'He told me that he was a detective,' the driver said. 'He told me to say nothing about what happened.'

'This is a serious matter,' Holmes warned the man. 'I want to know everything.'

'He gave me his name,' the driver said reluctantly. [1]

'That wasn't very intelligent of him,' Holmes commented. 'What name did he give you?

'Sherlock Holmes,' the driver replied. 'His name was Sherlock Holmes.'

Holmes was astonished [2] for a moment. Then he asked the driver where he took the passenger.

'I took him to Waterloo Station,' the driver said. 'He caught a train.'

Holmes gave the driver some money and sent him away. Then he turned to me seriously.

'Our enemy is clever, [3] Watson,' he told me. 'We don't know what he did in London. Be very careful at Baskerville Hall. There is great danger in this case.'

1. **reluctantly** : without wanting to.
2. **astonished** : greatly shocked.
3. **clever** : intelligent.

Go back to the text

1 Answer these questions.

a. What was Sir Henry's reaction when Holmes suggested that it could be too dangerous to go to Baskerville Hall? Angry

b. What did someone take from Sir Henry in the hotel? Shoe

c. What did Holmes do to see if Barrymore was in London? send a telegram

d. Who inherited most of Sir Charles's money? Henry

e. Who was Sir Charles's second brother? ~~Dad or Henry~~ Charle Roger

f. Who will inherit Sir Henry's money if he dies? James Desmond

g. Why couldn't Holmes come with Sir Henry to Baskerville Hall? had cases

h. Why did Holmes think that their enemy was very clever? He told to taxi he was sherlock holmes

T: GRADE 6

2 Topic – Travel

The Hound of the Baskervilles **takes place more than one hundred years ago. But already people could travel great distances fairly easily (at least compared to the 1700s!). There were already trains, steam-powered ships and underground railways (the first underground railway opened in 1863). Still, in the cities, people with some money went around in horse-drawn taxies.**

a. How do you think Sir Henry came from America to London?

b. How do you think Sir Henry will travel from London to his home in Devonshire?

c. How does the criminal follow Sir Henry in London?

3 Prepare a talk for your class about how people do the following things today:

- Move about large cities
- Travel from one city to another in the same country
- Travel from one side of the Atlantic Ocean to the other
- Why bicycles, horseback riding and walking are still very popular

4 **The words in this crossword puzzle all come from Chapters One to Three. Some are easy, some are hard, but all of them are to discover.**

Across

4. Something is .... that cannot be explained by logical, physical laws. (As Holmes says, a detective cannot investigate .... things.)
6. Holmes's profession.
8. The past simple of the verb 'to ride'.
9. A large amount of money is a ....
12. To stop being angry with somebody for something that he has done. (God will .... the innocent.)
14. Mr Sherlock Holmes smokes a ....
15. To not go near, to keep away from somebody or something. (The Baskervilles always .... the moors at night.)
16. To scare, to make somebody feel fear.
18. Very big.
19. You ring a .... or you knock to let the people in the house know that you have arrived.

Down

1. A dog used for hunting. It generally has short hair, floppy ears and a deep resonant bark.
2. A person who grows crops and raises animals. (The daughter of the .... was kidnapped by Sir Hugo.)
3. If you read .... , you say the words you are reading so that somebody else can hear them.
5. The opposite of fat.
7. The time between the afternoon and the night.
9. Mark your foot leaves in mud or snow.
10. The present simple of 'tore'.

11. Brave. (Baskerville hounds are usually very ....)

13. The organs of sight. (The .... of the Baskerville hound shone.)

14. To penalize, to hurt, to place in prison etc, somebody for having done something wrong. (Hugo Baskerville told his sons that God .... the wicked.)

17. The opposite of boy.

20. The opposite of above.

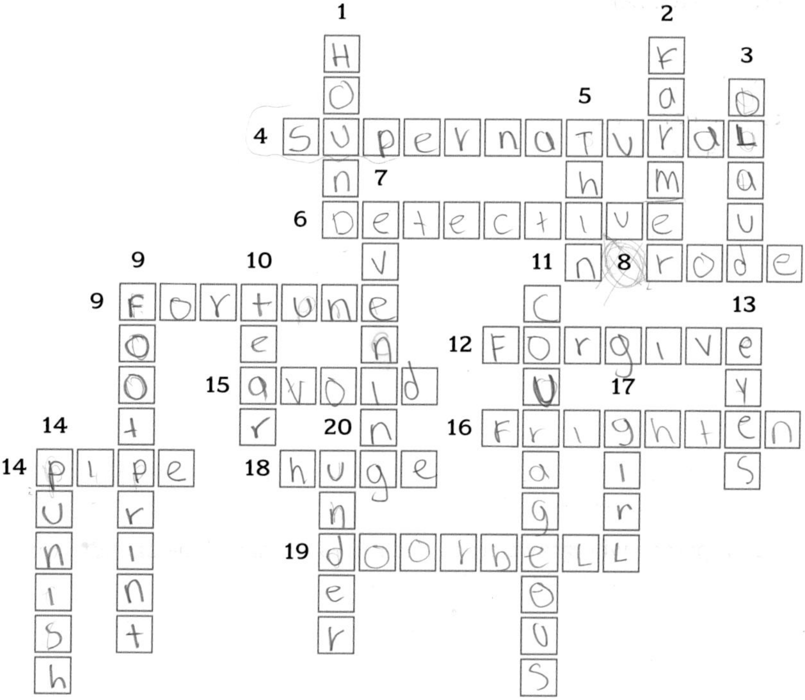

Early *Crime Detection*

Sherlock Holmes says that he is the 'only unofficial consulting detective' around. When the police cannot solve a crime he is called in, and with his unique skills and special knowledge he solves crimes. His special knowledge was indeed incredible for the time. He was an expert in handwriting, mud, [1] poisons, [2] anatomy and cigar ashes. He spent hours and hours reading about crimes of the past because he believed that there were no 'new crimes': there were, however, types of crimes that repeated themselves. In all this, Sherlock Holmes is a modern criminologist.

Real-life criminology began in the 1700s when the idea of crime was separated from the idea of religious sin [3] and was then studied as a separate phenomenon. By the 1800s criminologists began to distinguish their science from the new sciences of psychology and sociology, and to organise their own associations and to publish their own journals.

On the practical side of crime fighting, modern law enforcement [4] began in Great Britain when Sir Robert Peel, the Home Secretary, set up the Metropolitan Police Force in London in 1829. This was the world's first modern organised police force. Peel believed that this police force should be used to prevent crime, and that it should operate with the consent and cooperation of the public. At first

1. **mud** : mixture of earth and water.
2. **poisons** : substances that can kill.
3. **sin** : immoral action which breaks the law of God.
4. **law enforcement** : way of establishing the law.

people were sceptical [1] about it, but soon it was accepted and imitated all over Great Britain. It also became the model for modern police forces all around the world.

In 1842 the first Detective Department was established. It had only two inspectors and six sergeants. The British public, though, was very suspicious. In 1869 the Commissioner of Police wrote that for the majority of Englishmen, undercover [2] work is 'entirely foreign to the habits and feelings of the nation'.

A policeman on duty on a snowy night in a fashionable London square, from **The Graphic** 21st December 1872.

1. **sceptical** : untrusting.
2. **undercover** : secret work for investigation.

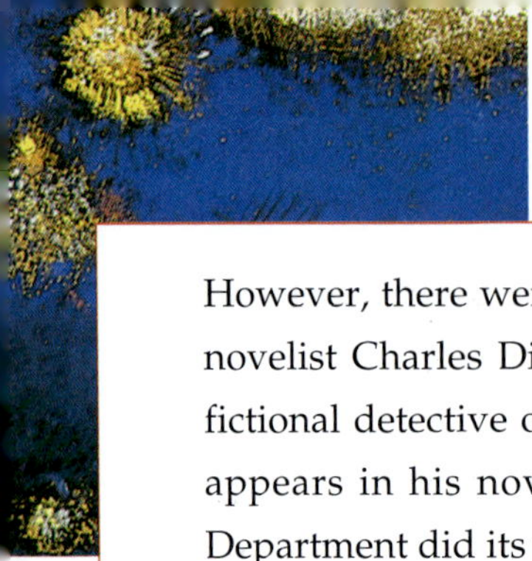

However, there were some supporters of undercover detectives. The novelist Charles Dickens was one of them, and he created the first fictional detective of the Metropolitan Police, Inspector Bucket, who appears in his novel *Bleak House*. Dickens felt that the Detective Department did its work extremely well.

In reality, there were many cases of corruption and incompetence. A good example of incompetence was the case of the infamous Jack the Ripper, which began in 1888. Besides its many mistakes, the department had one major problem: they refused to believe that a gentleman could be the murderer.

Holmes's scientific techniques were, in truth, at least ten years ahead of the time. In *A Study in Scarlet*, Holmes tells Watson that he has discovered a way of identifying bloodstains.[1] In the real world, such techniques were not developed until the early 1900s, some years after Austrian pathologist Karl Landsteiner had classified blood types in 1901.

One technique that was introduced during 'Holmes's lifetime' was the use of fingerprints[2] in solving crimes. It was developed by Sir Edward Henry. He had been the Inspector General of Police in Bengal, and used fingerprints to identify illiterate workers. When he became the head of the Criminal Investigation Department (CID), he immediately set up Scotland Yard's fingerprint section.

Once again, many people were not happy with this. One magistrate wrote to a newspaper: 'Scotland Yard, once known as the world's finest police organisation will be considered ridiculous if it uses fingerprints to convict criminals.'

1. **bloodstains** : marks made by blood.
2. **fingerprints** : marks made on a surface by fingers.

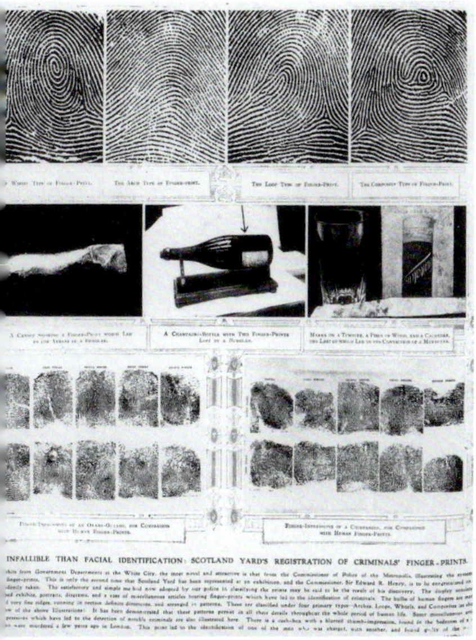

Fingerprinting (*c.* 1905)
from **Illustrated London News**.

But the first murder conviction based on fingerprints did happen. In 1905, brothers Alfred and Albert Stratton were convicted of murder. Alfred Stratton had left bloody fingerprints on the cash box of the shop. The lawyer who defended the brothers said that the use of fingerprints was more like 'French courts than of English justice' – a terrible insult at the time. The brothers were hanged anyway.

So, slowly but surely, the real world of criminal detection reached the levels of the imaginary Sherlock Holmes.

1 Answer the following questions.

do things police can't

a. What did an 'unofficial consulting detective' do?

expert in alot of things

b. What kinds of special knowledge did Sherlock Holmes have?

Identify bloodstains

c. Why did Sherlock Holmes study crimes of the past?

He belived crimes repeated

d. When was the first modern organised police force set up?

1829

e. What did Sir Robert Peel say was the purpose of the first organised police force? Used to provent crime

f. Who created the first fictional detective? Charles Dickens

g. How were the Detective Department's investigations of the case of Jack the Ripper limited? don't belive a gentleman can do it

h. Why did Sir Edward Henry first use fingerprints?

Identify illiterate workers

The Hound of the Baskervilles: the Film

Basil Rathbone as Sherlock Holmes
in the 1939 film version of **The Hound of the Baskervilles.**

Although there have been numerous film versions of *The Hound of the Baskervilles*, the most popular remains the 1939 production.

Try and find out:

- Who the main actors were
- How the film is different from book
- 'Who' played the hound

Before you read

PET 1 **Listen to the beginning of Chapter Four. You will hear Dr Watson describing his journey to and arrival at Baskerville Hall. For each question, fill in the missing information in the numbered space.**

5

The Departure

Dr Watson and Sir Henry left from **(1)** .... Station.

Holmes told Sir Henry not **(2)** .... He also told Watson that **(3)** .... with him.

The Arrival on the Moors

A **(4)** .... was waiting for them at the station.

While they were going to Baskerville Hall they saw a **(5)** .... standing in the road.

He was looking for a dangerous **(6)** ....

Baskerville Hall

(7) .... welcomed Sir Henry and Dr Watson on their arrival at Baskerville Hall.

Baskerville Hall was a **(8)** .... house.

CHAPTER **FOUR**

Sir Henry Baskerville Goes Home

We said goodbye to Holmes at Waterloo Station the next morning. Holmes once again told Sir Henry not to go onto the moors, and he said that I should carry my gun with me.

At last the train arrived at the moors. The countryside looked dark and frightening.

The carriage [1] from Baskerville Hall was there for us at the station. Soon we were driving along the narrow [2] roads. We turned a corner and saw a soldier standing in the road. He carried a rifle. [3] We stopped the carriage and Dr Mortimer asked the soldier what he was doing.

1. **carriage** : (here) vehicle powered by horses.
2. **narrow** : not wide, thin.
3. **rifle** : 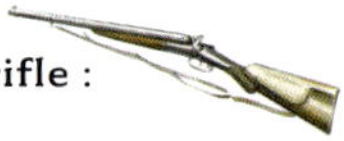

'A dangerous prisoner escaped three days ago,' the soldier explained. 'His name is Selden.'

I remembered the name from the newspaper stories. He was a cruel murderer.[1]

Now it began to grow dark and windy. It was cold as well. Finally we arrived at Baskerville Hall. It was a large house, and not a very cheerful[2] one. Barrymore came onto the steps of the Hall to welcome us.

'Welcome home, Sir Henry,' he said.

We ate together in the dining room, and the family pictures of the Baskervilles looked down on us from the walls. The atmosphere was not very happy.

After dinner I went to bed but it was difficult to sleep. Suddenly I heard the sound of a woman — she was crying desperately.

I told Sir Henry about the woman the next morning. He sent for Barrymore and he asked the butler about it. I noticed that Barrymore went white in the face before he answered.

'There are two women in the house, Sir,' he told Sir Henry. 'One of them is the maid.[3] The other is my wife. Mrs Barrymore was not crying last night.'

I knew that Barrymore was lying. I saw his wife later in the morning and her face was red. She looked very sad. I did not understand why Barrymore did not tell the truth and I felt suspicious of him. I decided to go to the post office to ask some questions about the telegram that Holmes had sent from London.

I found the boy who delivered the telegrams.

1. **murderer** : killer.
2. **cheerful** : happy, positive.
3. **maid** : woman servant.

'There was a telegram for Mr Barrymore from London yesterday,' I reminded him. 'Did you give it to Mr Barrymore yourself?'

'No, Sir,' the boy replied. 'They told me Mr Barrymore was up in the loft.[1] I gave the telegram to Mrs Barrymore.'

'I see,' I said. 'Did you see Mr Barrymore in the loft?'

'No, I didn't,' the boy admitted. 'But his wife told me he was there.'

Now it was impossible to tell if Barrymore was the passenger in the taxi, or whether he stayed at Baskerville Hall that day.

I was walking away from the post office when a man stopped me. He told me that his name was Stapleton, and that he was a friend of Dr Mortimer. He had a butterfly net[2] with him.

'You must be Dr Watson,' he said. 'Dr Mortimer told me about you. I know that you're also a friend of the great detective Sherlock Holmes. Is he going to come here as well?'

'I'm afraid not,' I replied. 'Sherlock Holmes is working on another case in London.'

'What a pity,' Mr Stapleton said politely. 'Still, I hope you'll come home with me and meet my sister. She'll be pleased to see you.'

I accepted Mr Stapleton's invitation. We walked to his house together. Stapleton told me a little about himself. He said that he and his sister had moved to the moors two years ago. He liked the moors, he said.

'Look over there,' he pointed. 'That place is called Great

1. **loft** : space inside the roof of a house.

2. **butterfly net** :

Grimpen Marsh. [1] If an animal or a man goes there, they never come out. The ground is very soft and they sink down [2] inside it. But I know how to cross the moors safely,' he told me proudly. 'There are some paths among the marshes.'

While Mr Stapleton was talking I saw a horse on the edge of the marsh. The poor animal was half under water. It struggled furiously [3] to get free – but the water closed over its head.

'Another one dead,' Stapleton commented sadly. 'It happens all the time on the moors, Dr Watson.'

Then we heard a terrible cry over the marshes. It was a very deep and sad cry. I looked at Stapleton in surprise.

'What was that?' I asked him.

'People say that that is the Hound of the Baskervilles,' he told me.

'You don't surely believe in the stories about the Hound of the Baskervilles, Mr Stapleton?' I asked him in surprise. 'You're an educated man!'

'I think it was a bird. There are some very rare birds on the moors.'

Just then a butterfly flew past us. Mr Stapleton ran after it with his net. He ran straight onto the marsh. He was not afraid.

I was watching him when a beautiful young woman with dark skin and eyes came up to me.

'Go back to London,' she said quietly. 'Ssh! Don't say a word. My brother's coming back!'

Mr Stapleton came off the marsh and joined us. He did not seem pleased that we were talking together.

1. **marsh** : area of wet, dangerous ground.
2. **sink down** : (sink, sank, sunk) move down.
3. **struggled furiously** : made a great effort.

'Hello, dear,' he said to his sister. 'I see that you have met our guest.'

'Yes,' she replied. 'I told Sir Henry that the marsh is not very beautiful at this time of year.'

'I'm not Sir Henry,' I corrected her. 'I'm Dr Watson, a friend of his.'

The woman looked embarrassed.

'Please forget what I told you,' she said very quietly.

The three of us walked to their house, Merripit House. Stapleton talked about his love for the moors. He told me about the animals and plants that fascinated him in that part of the country. We talked together for a while and then I left them to go back to Baskerville Hall.

Miss Stapleton was waiting for me further down the road.

'Please forget what I said,' she said again. 'I did not mean anything terrible.'

'But you believe Sir Henry is in danger?' I asked her.

'I believe in the story of the Hound of the Baskervilles,' she told me. 'That is why I said what I did.'

'Why didn't you want your brother to hear what you said?' I persisted.

'My brother wants Sir Henry to live at Baskerville Hall,' she explained. 'He does not want Sir Henry to go away because of these silly[1] stories. That's why he does not want me to talk about the Hound of the Baskervilles.'

1. **silly** : ridiculous.

Go back to the text

1 Match the phrases in columns A and B to make complete sentences that are correct within the context of the story.

A

a. Barrymore went white in the face
b. Dr Watson understood that Barrymore was lying
c. Dr Watson could not be certain that Barrymore was not in London
d. The horse died
e. Miss Stapleton became embarrassed after telling Watson to go back to London
f. Mr Stapleton was not very pleased
g. Mr Stapleton loved the moors
h. Miss Stapleton said that she wanted Sir Henry to leave the moors
i. Mr Stapleton did not want Sir Henry to leave Baskerville Hall

B

1. [C] because the boy did not give the telegram to Mr Barrymore himself.
2. [F] because Watson was talking to his sister.
3. [h] because she believed in the story of the hound.
4. [I] because of silly stories about huge hounds.
5. [a] because Sir Henry asked him about the woman crying in the night.
6. [e] because she had thought he was Sir Henry.
7. [d] because it fell into the marsh.
8. [g] because he was extremely interested in the plants and animals that lived there.
9. [b] because his wife's face was red and she looked very sad.

'I was walking away from the post office when a man stopped me'

The **Past Continuous** tells us about what was happening at a certain time in the past.

*Last week at this time, I **was skiing** in the Alps.*

*I walked into the living room. My brother **was sleeping** on the sofa; my mother and father **were playing** cards; and Hubert, our cat, **was looking** out of the window.*

Often the Past Continuous is contrasted with the Past Simple. In this case, the Past Continuous gives us the background to the action or event described by the Past Simple.

*I **was sleeping** when the phone **rang**.*

*While I **was walking** out on the moors I **saw** a huge black hound.*

Notice the difference in meaning between the following two sentences.

*When I **arrived** home my mother **was cooking** dinner. = I arrived home and my mother was cooking dinner.* (She had started to cook before I arrived.)

*When I **arrived** home my mother **cooked** dinner. = I arrived home and then* (after I arrived) *my mother started to cook dinner.*

2 Put the verbs in brackets in the Past Simple or Past Continuous according to the context.

a. While we .... (*travel*) to Baskerville Hall I .... (*see*) a soldier near the road. He .... (*look*) for a dangerous murderer.

b. What .... (*you/do*) when Mum .... (*come*) home?

c. While I .... (*clean*) my room I .... (*find*) a photo of my first girlfriend under the bed in an old notebook.

d. Constance: What .... (*you/do*) when the teacher .... (*come*) into the classroom?
Kevin: I .... (*play*) cards with Christian.

e. I .... (*break*) my wife's favourite glass while I .... (*wash up*).

f. I .... (*see*) Watson yesterday afternoon. He .... (*walk*) across the moors.

g. I .... (*think*) about John when he .... (*knock*) on the door.

h. While Jennifer .... (*watch*) TV last night, she .... (*hear*) a strange noise outside her window.

'He had a butterfly net with him'

In English nouns can qualify or describe other nouns. In other words, nouns are often used as adjectives.

When a noun is used to qualify another noun the two words together are called a **compound noun**.

In general nouns are used as adjectives when we want to say:

- what an object is used for: *a butterfly net, a dinner table, an emergency exit, a tennis court*
- what an object is made of: *a cotton shirt, a brick house, a gold watch, a diamond ring*
- where something is located: *a country road, a village café, a city street, a mountain resort*
- when something happens or appears: *a morning newspaper, a spring shower, an evening newspaper, a summer cold*
- when we talk about sports, hobbies and jobs: *a chess game, water skiing, a rugby match, a sheep farmer*

3 Use the nouns in the box to form compound nouns to fill in the gaps

guitar	**lake**	**morning**	**kitchen**	**summer**
table	**player**	**mountain**	**paper**	**romance**

1. We are starting a rock band. We have a drummer and two singers. Now we need a good ....
2. We spend each summer in the Alps by a beautiful ...., where I go fishing.
3. George and I met by the sea during our vacation and fell in love. Everybody said it was just a ...., but in the end, we married and are very happy together.
4. When I get up I have a cup of coffee and read the ....
5. The butter is over there on the .... next to glasses.

CHAPTER **FIVE**

Mr Stapleton and his Sister

Mr Stapleton came to Baskerville Hall to meet Sir Henry, and the two men became friends. We all met every day. I noticed that Sir Henry was in love with Miss Stapleton. Her brother did not seem to like this, and he tried to keep them apart.

I met a friend of Sir Henry's called Frankland. Frankland was an old man who loved two things. He loved to argue, [1] and he loved to study the moors through a large telescope. Frankland was sure that he could detect the escaped prisoner Selden with his telescope.

1. **argue** : (here) debate.

I woke up very late one night because I heard a noise outside my bedroom. I got up very quietly and opened the door. Barrymore was in the corridor with a candle in his hand. He went into an empty bedroom and stood near the window. He held the candle against the glass. I went back to my own room. He did not see me.

I told Sir Henry the next morning about Barrymore.

'Tonight we'll follow him together,' Sir Henry decided. 'I want to find out what he's doing!'

That night we followed Barrymore. He went into the same empty bedroom with a candle. Again he stood near the window with the candle in his hand.

'What are you doing, Barrymore?' Sir Henry asked sternly. [1]

Barrymore was surprised to see Sir Henry and me.

'I wanted to be sure the window was closed, Sir,' he said.

'I think you sent a signal,' I told him. 'Give me that candle.'

I took the candle from Barrymore and held it against the glass. Immediately we saw a light on the moor.

'There!' I cried.

'What's all this about?' [2] Sir Henry asked angrily.

Barrymore did not reply.

'I can tell you, Sir,' said a woman's voice. We turned to see Mrs Barrymore behind us.

'It's my poor brother out there on the moors. He's the escaped prisoner. We show him the light when we have food ready for him. He shows us where to put the food with his light.'

Sir Henry thought for a moment then he spoke to Barrymore.

1. **sternly** : seriously.
2. **what's all this about?** : what's happening here?

'You're trying to help your wife,' he said. 'I cannot blame[1] you for that. Go to bed now and we'll talk about this tomorrow.'

Barrymore and his wife went to their room.

'Let's see if we can catch this Selden,' Sir Henry suggested. 'He's out on the moor somewhere.'

Sir Henry and I left the house together. We walked towards the point where we had seen the light on the moor. Suddenly we heard the very deep and sad cry. Sir Henry looked afraid for a moment but he continued walking.

Soon we came to the place where the light was. There was a candle on a rock. We saw a man behind the rock. He had a terrible face. When he saw us he began to run away.

'Selden!' cried Sir Henry.

We ran after him. Selden ran very quickly and we could not catch him. Then a strange thing happened. There was a moon that night, and we saw another man in the moonlight. He was standing on top of a small hill. He seemed to watch Selden, Sir Henry and myself. Who was this mysterious stranger? Was he a friend or an enemy? I decided to take Sir Henry back to Baskerville Hall immediately for his own safety.

The next morning Sir Henry and Barrymore spoke about Selden. Sir Henry wanted to catch him and give him to the police, but Barrymore wanted him to go free.

'He's a murderer,' Sir Henry reminded him.

'I know, Sir,' Barrymore admitted. 'But he's not dangerous any more. And soon he'll be on a boat to South America. We've organised his escape for him.'

1. **blame** : criticise.

'Very well, Barrymore, I won't look for him again,' Sir Henry promised. 'I don't want you and your wife to get into trouble.'

'Thank you, Sir,' Barrymore said. 'You're helping me, and I can help you in return. I know something about Sir Charles's death.'

'What do you know?' Sir Henry cried impatiently.

'I know why he went to the Yew Alley,' Barrymore replied. 'He was going to meet a woman there.'

'How do you know this?' Sir Henry asked.

'Sir Charles received a letter the day of his death,' Barrymore told us. 'He threw it into the fire, but one page did not burn. My wife read what it said: "Burn the letter. Meet me at the gate at ten o'clock. L. L." The handwriting was a woman's, Sir.'

Later I asked Dr Mortimer if he knew a woman with the initials 'L. L.'

'Of course I do,' he said. 'It's Mrs Laura Lyons — she's Frankland's daughter. She married a bad man who left her. She and her father quarrelled.[1] The poor woman lives alone. She tries to make money with her typewriter.[2] It's a sad story. Both her husband and her father treated her badly.'

The other thing that happened that day was this. I wanted to know if Selden was still on the moors, so I asked Barrymore.

'I don't know, Sir,' he told me. 'We leave food for him as always, and someone takes it. But we don't know if it's him or the other man who takes it.'

'You know there's another man out there?' I asked. 'How do you know that?'

1. **quarrelled** : had a bad disagreement.

2. **typewriter** : 

'Selden told us,' Barrymore explained. 'He saw him. He said the other man lives in one of the huts [1] on the moors. A boy brings him food.'

I thought about this mysterious man who lived out on the moors by himself. I decided to look for him myself. I did not want to ask Sir Henry to go with me. He was already in enough danger. I decided to go by myself.

1. **huts** : 

Go back to the text

PET **1** **For each question, mark the letter next to the correct answer – A, B, C or D.**

1 When Mr Stapleton realised that Sir Henry was in love with Miss Stapleton he

- **A** ☐ often brought her to Baskerville Hall to see Sir Henry.
- **B** ☐ became friends with Sir Henry.
- **C** ☒ didn't want them to see each other.
- **D** ☐ stopped coming to see Sir Henry at Baskerville Hall.

2 Barrymore was standing in front of the window with a candle because

- **A** ☒ he wanted to send a signal to his wife's brother.
- **B** ☐ he thought he could see the escaped prisoner on the moor.
- **C** ☐ he was listening to hear the sound of the woman crying.
- **D** ☐ he wanted to send a signal to his wife to tell her where to take the food.

3 Sir Henry looked afraid for a moment when he heard the cry on the moor because he thought it was

- **A** ☐ a mysterious woman.
- **B** ☒ the Hound of the Baskervilles.
- **C** ☐ the escaped prisoner.
- **D** ☐ someone who had fallen into the marsh.

4 Sir Henry decided to stop looking for Selden because

- **A** ☐ he was afraid of the mysterious man out on the moors.
- **B** ☐ Selden planned to leave England anyway.
- **C** ☐ he did not want the Barrymores to get into trouble.
- **D** ☒ he did not want the Barrymores to get into trouble and Selden planned to go to South America.

5 Sir Charles went to the gate on the day of his death because

- A ☐ he was bringing food to Selden.
- B ☐ he wanted to smoke his cigar in peace.
- C ☒ he planned to meet Laura Lyons.
- D ☐ he planned to meet Miss Stapleton.

PET **2 Mrs Barrymore receives this note from her brother.**

> Dear sister,
>
> I saw your husband with the candle, and then I saw another man with him and then another! Is something wrong? Will you continue to bring me food? Should I escape immediately?
>
> Please answer me quickly.
>
> Your miserably sad brother,
>
> Selden

Write a short letter from Mrs Barrymore to comfort your brother in about 100 words. Explain:

- how Sir Henry discovered that they were taking food
- why Sir Henry stopped searching for him
- how they helped Sir Henry

You can begin you letter like this:

> My dearest brother,
>
> I know you must be very frightened...

PET **3** **Read the summary of Chapters One to Five and choose the correct word for each space. For each question, write the letter – A, B, C or D.**

(0) .... morning Dr Mortimer came to visit Sherlock Holmes for **(1)** .... advice. Dr Mortimer's friend Sir Charles Baskerville had died three months earlier, and there was something strange **(2)** .... his death. The newspapers said that Sir Charles had died from a weak heart, but Dr Mortimer was not sure.

Baskerville Hall was located out on the moors. There was a frightening legend about a terrible supernatural hound **(3)** .... lived there. This hound, it seems, had killed one of Sir Charles's ancestors, the cruel Sir Hugo. **(4)** .... then, other members of the Baskerville family had died in mysterious **(5)** ...., and Dr Mortimer did not want **(6)** .... terrible to **(7)** .... to Sir Charles's heir, Sir Henry. Sir Henry had lived in America and had just arrived in London.

The next day Holmes met Sir Henry. Sir Henry showed him a note he had received. It said, 'Don't go to the moor. Your life is in danger.' **(8)** .... Sir Henry refused to be frightened away from his own home, Holmes decided to send Watson with him to Baskerville Hall on the moors.

When they arrived **(9)** .... Baskerville Hall, Watson encountered some strange people. He met Mr Stapleton who loved the plants and animals of the moors and Mr Frankland who loved to argue and look out across the moors with his telescope. Watson discovered that the brother of the butler's wife was an escaped murderer who was hiding out on the moors, and that Mr Frankland's daughter, Laura Lyons, had asked Sir Henry to meet her on the night of his death. Then, to make things **(10)** .... more complicated, there was a mysterious stranger who lived in a hut out on the moors as well. So, Watson decided he would go and see who that mysterious stranger was.

0	**A** A	**B** The	**C** This	**D** One
1	**A** the	**B** some	**C** an	**D** some
2	**A** about	**B** around	**C** concerned	**D** on
3	**A** what	**B** who	**C** that	**D** whom
4	**A** From	**B** Of	**C** Since	**D** Until
5	**A** fashions	**B** manners	**C** style	**D** ways
6	**A** anything	**B** something	**C** nothing	**D** things
7	**A** occur	**B** come	**C** go	**D** happen
8	**A** However	**B** Since	**C** For	**D** Given
9	**A** to	**B** on	**C** at	**D** in
10	**A** very	**B** even	**C** much	**D** especially

Before you read

PET 1 7 **You will hear a conversation between Dr Watson and Mrs Laura Lyons about her letter to Sir Charles. Decide if each sentence is correct or incorrect. If it is correct, put a tick (✓) in the box under A for YES. If it is not correct, put a tick (✓) in the box under B for NO.**

		A	B
1	At first Mrs Lyons said she did not write to Sir Charles.	☐	☐
2	Watson told her that one of the servants had found a page of the letter.	☐	☐
3	Mrs Lyons wanted to ask Sir Charles advice about divorcing her husband.	☐	☐
4	Mrs Lyons wanted to meet Sir Charles in the garden because she did not want her husband see her in the house.	☐	☐
5	Mrs Lyons did not go to see Sir Charles because she decided not to divorce her husband.	☐	☐
6	Mrs Lyons sent Sir Charles a telegram to explain why she did not come to see him.	☐	☐

CHAPTER **SIX**

Mrs Laura Lyons Tells All

I went to visit Mrs Laura Lyons at her house in Coombe Tracey. She was a beautiful young lady. I told her that I wanted to help Sir Henry Baskerville.

'I want to ask you about Sir Charles,' I told her. 'I understand that you wrote to him the day he died. Why did you want to meet him?'

Mrs Lyons was very angry.

'I don't know what you're talking about!' she said.

'I know you wrote to him,' I told her calmly. 'You wrote: "Burn the letter. Meet me at the gate at ten o'clock. L. L." Sir Charles burnt the letter, but one of the servants found a page from it in the fireplace. Why did you want to see him, Mrs Lyons?'

Mrs Lyons was very red in the face.

'I needed his help,' she said quietly. 'I married a bad man and I wanted a divorce. I wanted to ask Sir Charles's advice. I asked

him to meet me in the garden because I did not want his servants to see me in the house. I did not want them to talk about me.'

'I understand,' I said. 'Now tell me what happened when you saw Sir Charles.'

'I didn't see him,' Mrs Lyons said. 'Someone else gave me the help I wanted. I wanted to write to him to explain but then I heard he was dead.'

Next I decided it was time to find the mysterious man who lived on the moors. I followed a path that went near Mr Frankland's house. He saw me and came out to talk. He was very angry with the police, he told me.

'I'm trying to help them find the murderer Selden,' he said. 'I don't know where he's hiding, but I'm watching the boy who takes him his food. I'm watching him with my telescope, you see. But the police aren't interested. Come with me a moment. The boy delivers the murderer's food about now. You'll see everything!'

I went into Mr Frankland's house. There was a large telescope on the roof. Mr Frankland looked through it eagerly. [1]

'Ah!' he cried happily. 'I can see the boy now. You have a look.'

I looked through the instrument, and I could see a boy walking on the moors. He was carrying a parcel. The boy disappeared over a hill.

I thanked Mr Frankland and walked quickly towards the hill. It was nearly dark when I reached the top of the hill. I looked down but I could not see anyone. There was a group of huts on the other side of the hill.

1. **eagerly** : enthusiastically.

One of the huts seemed in better condition than the others. I took out my revolver [1] and walked towards it. The hut was empty, but it was clear that someone used it. There were some blankets [2] on the floor and some pots [3] for cooking. The mysterious man was hiding here!

Suddenly there were footsteps in the darkness outside. I waited inside the hut with my revolver ready. I was frightened. The figure of a man appeared in the doorway of the hut.

'What a lovely evening, Watson,' said Sherlock Holmes.

'Holmes!' I cried. 'What are you doing here? I thought you were in London.'

'I wanted you to think that,' he told me. 'We have a dangerous enemy here, and I did not want you to know where I was.'

Then we began to discuss the case together.

'Did you know that Mrs Laura Lyons and Stapleton are very good friends?' he asked me. 'I wonder if Stapleton's wife knows about their friendship.'

'Stapleton hasn't got a wife,' I interrupted him, 'he lives with his sister.'

'He tells everyone that she is his sister,' Holmes told me, 'but I've checked – she's really Mrs Stapleton.'

'Why did Stapleton let Sir Henry fall in love with his wife?' I asked.

'Stapleton wanted to be close to Sir Henry,' Holmes explained. 'Having a beautiful sister made that possible for him, don't you see?'

1. **revolver** : type of gun, similar to a pistol.
2. **blankets** : 
3. **pots** : 

'So Stapleton's the enemy,' I guessed. 'He's the man who followed us to London, and his wife wrote the warning note to Sir Henry!'

'Yes,' agreed Holmes.

'But why are Stapleton and Mrs Lyons good friends if Stapleton already has a wife?' I asked him.

'Mrs Lyons does not know that Stapleton is already married,' Sherlock Holmes told me. 'She's in love with him. She wants a divorce because she wants to marry him. And he pretends that he wants to marry her. I think she'll help us when she knows the whole truth!'

'And what about Stapleton?' I asked my friend. 'What does he want?'

'Murder, my friend,' Holmes told me grimly.[1] 'And I hope I'm going to catch him before he does it.'

Just then we heard the deep and sad cry out on the moors. Holmes looked pale for a second then he stood up.

'Where is it, Watson? Where is it?' he cried.

We heard the same cry several times. Then we heard a new noise. It was terrible. Holmes moved forward.

'The hound, Watson, the hound!'

He ran into the darkness.

1. **grimly** : very seriously.

Go back to the text

1 Answer the following questions.

a. Where did Sir Charles and Laura plan to meet? Gate

b. What did Mr Frankland show Watson? The boy who stole food

c. Who was the mysterious man on the moors? Holmes

d. Why did Mr Stapleton say that his wife is his sister? want to be close with Sir Henry

e. Who did Mrs Lyons want to marry? Stapleton

f. Why will Laura Lyons help Holmes catch Mr Stapleton? Is in love

g. What did Holmes and Watson hear? The hound

'I told her that I wanted to help Sir Henry Baskerville'

When we say what somebody said we can use that person's exact words.
And then John said, 'I am not feeling very well.'

Or we can use **reported speech**.
And then John said that he was not feeling very well.

Look at the changes that occur when you change a statement from direct to reported speech.

Direct speech	Reported speech
'***My*** girlfriend ***is*** in London,' said John	John said that ***his*** girlfriend ***was*** in London.
'***My*** brother ***is playing*** football,' said Paul.	Paul said that ***his*** brother ***was playing*** football.
'I ***am going to see*** her ***tomorrow***,' said Mary.	Mary said that ***she was going to see*** her ***the next day***.
'They ***have*** already ***had*** dinner,' said Georgia.	Georgia said that they ***had*** already ***had*** dinner.
'I ***went*** to the post office ***yesterday***,' said Morgan.	Morgan said that he ***had gone*** to the post office ***the day before***.
'I ***cannot come this*** evening,' said Watson.	Watson said that he ***could not come that*** evening.
'We ***will arrive next week***,' said Emily.	Emily said that they ***would arrive the following week***.

2 **Change the following statements into reported speech.**

a. 'I am Dr Mortimer,' said the young man.
b. 'I need your advice,' said Dr Mortimer to Mr Holmes.
c. 'We will help you,' said Mr Holmes.
d. 'There are certain things that I cannot believe,' said Dr Mortimer.
e. 'Barrymore found Sir Charles's body,' said Dr Mortimer.
f. 'You're a good observer,' said Holmes.
g. 'I am going to make your dinner tonight,' said his father.
h. 'I am studying for my English examination,' said Louis.

3 **Change the following into direct speech.**

a. They said that they had seen a huge animal on the moor.
b. Harriet said that she was going to call her brother the next day.
c. Tommy said that he could not speak French very well.
d. Mr Holmes said that he had not understood his friend's explanation.
e. Jane said she would help mother tomorrow.
f. She said she always had her breakfast at 8 o'clock.
g. Brian said that he had eaten with his classmates the day before.
h. Margaret said that she did not know anything about computers.

a. They have seen a huge animal on the moor
b. She is going to call her brother the next day
c. he can not speak French very well
d. He hasn't understood his friend's explanation
e. She will help mother tomorrow
f. She always has her breakfast at 8 o'clock
g. He ate with his classment yesterday
h. She doesn't know anything abut

Before you read

PET **1** **Listen to Chapter Seven. For each question put a tick (✓) in the correct box.**

8

1 First Watson heard some more screams and then they heard

A ☐ something hit the ground.
B ☐ somebody shouting for help.
C ☐ a hound barking.

2 After he examined the body, Holmes began to

A ☐ cry.
B ☐ call for help.
C ☐ laugh.

3 Stapleton said that he was worried about Sir Henry because

A ☐ Sir Henry had left his house early.
B ☐ Sir Henry was invited to his house but never arrived.
C ☐ he had heard the hound barking.

4 Holmes tells Selden that he is returning to London

A ☐ that evening.
B ☐ in two days.
C ☐ tomorrow.

5 Tomorrow Sir Henry is going

A ☐ to London.
B ☐ to Stapleton's house for dinner.
C ☐ to see Laura Lyons.

CHAPTER **SEVEN**

Death on the Moor

We ran together through the darkness. We heard some more terrible screams. Then we heard something hit the ground.

'We're too late, Watson!' Holmes told me desperately. 'But if Sir Henry is dead, I shall bring justice to Stapleton in the end!'

We came to the edge of a small cliff [1] on the moor. We stopped here and looked over into the darkness. There was a body on the moor below us. It was Sir Henry and he was dead.

'It's my fault!' [2] I told Holmes. 'You instructed me to stay with Sir Henry and now he's dead. It's all my fault.'

'The fault is mine,' Holmes said grimly. 'I knew who the murderer was, and I thought I could catch him before he killed. It

1. **edge... cliff** : end of an area of high ground.
2. **fault** : responsibility.

is the biggest mistake of my career. But why did Sir Henry come onto the moor?'

Holmes climbed down the cliff and examined the body carefully. Suddenly he began to laugh loudly. He called me to him.

'It's not Sir Henry,' he said happily, 'it's not Sir Henry. Look at the face, Watson! It's Selden. Selden's got a beard and he's wearing Sir Henry's clothes.'

Holmes thought for a moment.

'I know what happened,' he said. 'Sir Henry gave some old clothes to Barrymore to throw away. Barrymore gave them to Selden — and the hound followed Sir Henry's scent [1] and killed him,' he paused. 'But how did Selden know that the hound was after him? He screamed for a long time.'

'There's something else I don't understand,' I told Holmes. 'Why did Stapleton let the hound onto the moor tonight? Did he think Sir Henry was out tonight?'

'We'll soon know,' Holmes announced. 'Stapleton is over there. Now we must try and prove that he is guilty.'

He pointed to a man who we saw in the darkness.

'Don't let him think we suspect him,' Holmes whispered [2] urgently.

'Is that you, Dr Watson?' Stapleton called out. He walked closer. 'Has there been an accident? Is that Sir Henry?'

He examined the body of the criminal.

'Who is this?' he asked me in great surprise.

'It's the escaped prisoner Selden,' I explained.

1. **scent** : smell.
2. **whispered** : said very quietly.

'I heard something. That's why I came onto the moor,' Stapleton explained. 'I'm worried about Sir Henry. I invited him to my house this evening but he didn't arrive. That's why I'm here.'

Stapleton looked closely at Holmes.

'Did you hear anything strange?' he asked.

'No,' replied Holmes. 'What do you mean?'

'The stories about the Hound of the Baskervilles. Anything like that?'

'We did not hear anything like that,' I replied.

'How did this man die?' Stapleton asked.

'He fell over the cliff,' I said.

'Do you agree with that, Mr Sherlock Holmes?' Stapleton asked my friend.

'You know who I am,' Holmes replied quietly.

'We've all been expecting you,' Stapleton told him. 'We know that you and Dr Watson are close friends.'

'Selden's death is a sad event but it will not stop me returning to London tomorrow,' Holmes said.

'Will you tell us about the strange things here on the moors?' Stapleton asked him.

'This is not a good case for me,' Holmes replied. 'There are a lot of stories about supernatural hounds – but a detective needs facts, not stories.'

Stapleton studied my friend's face. Holmes seemed to be telling the truth.

'I must go home, gentlemen,' he told us. He walked away into the darkness.

Holmes and I walked back to Baskerville Hall.

'We still have no evidence against Stapleton,' Holmes reminded me. 'Sir Charles died because of his heart and Selden fell over the cliff. Don't say very much to Sir Henry about Selden's death. Don't mention the hound. I've got a plan for tomorrow and I don't want Sir Henry to be anxious. He will need his courage tomorrow. I think you told me that he was going to the Stapletons' house for dinner tomorrow evening?'

'That's right,' I agreed. 'They invited me as well.'

'I want him to go alone,' Holmes said.

Go back to the text

PET 1 Decide if each statement is correct or incorrect. If it is correct, mark A. If it is not correct, mark B.

		A	B
1	At first, Holmes thought that Watson was responsible for Sir Henry's death.	☐	☐
2	The hound ran after Selden because he was wearing Sir Henry's clothes.	☐	☐
3	Stapleton was happy that Selden was dead and not Sir Henry.	☐	☐
4	The hound killed Selden.	☐	☐
5	Stapleton did not recognise Holmes.	☐	☐
6	Holmes was not interested in investigating the death of Selden.	☐	☐
7	Holmes did not think that Stapleton was responsible for the death of Sir Charles.	☐	☐
8	Holmes did not want Sir Henry to know how Selden really died.	☐	☐

Now correct the incorrect statements.

PET 2 Here are some sentences from Chapters Five to Seven. For each question, complete the second sentence so that it means the same as the first, using no more than three words.

0 Selden ran very quickly and we could not catch him.
Selden ran ..*so quickly*.............. that we could not catch him.

1 I have some knowledge about Sir Charles's death.
I know .... Sir Charles's death.

2 The poor woman lives alone.
The poor woman .... with anybody.

3 Sir Charles burnt the letter, but one of the servants found a page from it in the fireplace.
One of the servants found a page from the letter in the fireplace, ... Sir Charles had burnt the letter.

4 I wanted to write to him to explain but then I heard he was dead.
I did not write to him to explain .... he was already dead.

5 We did not hear anything like that.
We heard .... like that.

3 **Find the opposites of the following words in this chapter.**

a. alive ....
b. beginning ....
c. large ....
d. light ....
e. above ....
f. carelessly ....
g. softly ....
h. new ....
i. happy ....

4 **Now fill in the gaps with one of the words given above or one of the opposites you have found.**

1. When Sir Henry looked out the window into the ......darkness........, he saw the light of Selden's candle.
2. Holmes was very .... when he discovered that Sir Henry was not dead.
3. When Sir Henry was in the hotel in London somebody took one of his .... shoes, and then somebody took one of his .... shoes.
4. Watson could not sleep during his first night at Baskerville Hall because he heard a woman crying ....
5. Selden thought he was going to escape to South America but in the .... he died in England.
6. The legend tells of an incredibly .... hound that killed the evil Sir Hugo.

The Coming of *the Fairies*

In *The Hound of the Baskervilles* when Dr Mortimer says that perhaps there really is a supernatural hound, Sherlock Holmes becomes quite annoyed. He says, 'I see that you have quite gone over to [1] the supernaturalists. But now, Dr Mortimer, tell me this. If you hold these views why have you come to consult me at all?' The whole novel is particularly interesting because it shows how an intelligent criminal uses an old legend about the supernatural to confuse people and commit his crimes.

What is even more fascinating is the fact that Sir Arthur Conan Doyle, the creator of Sherlock Holmes, really *did* believe in the supernatural. What is more, Conan Doyle spent the last years of his life promoting, with his time and money, the cause of Spiritualism. He also believed in the existence of fairies.

These facts have embarrassed many fans of the great scientific detective, and some have said that Conan Doyle was more like Dr Watson than Sherlock Holmes.

Others have tried to explain Doyle's belief in the spirit world with the death of his beloved son Kingsley during the First World War. Certainly, an interest in communicating with the dead increased after that war: many parents and wives were desperate for one last chance to communicate with their dead sons and husbands.

Still, this does not really explain Conan Doyle's interest. First of all, he announced his conversion to Spiritualism in 1916, two years

1. **have... over to** : you agree with.

The Fox Sisters. The renowned spiritual mediums Margaret Fox and her sister Catherine Fox with Mrs Fish.

before his son's death, and he had been interested in Spiritualism since as early as 1886.

Spiritualism, like many other religions, professes a belief in life after death. Unlike other religions, though, it says that it can provide tangible evidence that we can communicate with the dead. In this way, it is a religion of our modern scientific world.

Spiritualism itself began in 1848 when three teenage girls (the Fox sisters) from Hydesville, New York, said they heard the sounds of spirits in their house. They began to respond to the sounds of the ghosts with clapping, [1] and then they developed a code to actually communicate with the spirits. They also said that they spoke with the spirit of a travelling tradesman who had been murdered in their house. Later, when they found a skeleton in their cellar, the three girls became celebrities and modern Spiritualism was born.

Directly connected with Conan Doyle's belief in Spiritualism was his belief in the Cottingley Fairies.

In 1917 two girls from the town of Cottingley in Yorkshire took pictures of fairies. Some photographic experts declared that the photos were not fakes. Conan Doyle himself became involved, and even wrote a book supporting the photos. This book *The Coming of*

Frances Griffiths and the Cottingley Fairies in a photograph taken in 1917.

1. **clapping**: hitting hands together to make a noise.

the Fairies was ridiculed by many. But Conan Doyle, who was generally a kind, good-humoured man, never seemed to mind. He believed that the 'photographic proof' of the existence of fairies would make people believe in Spiritualism.

So, in the end, it is not so strange that the inventor of Sherlock Holmes was a convinced Spiritualist and believed in fairies. This is just further proof of the power of Conan Doyle's imaginary creation, Sherlock Holmes, a creation that seems to many as real as any person they have ever known.

1 Say whether the following statements are true (T) or false (F), and then correct the false ones.

	T	F
a. Sherlock Holmes became annoyed with Dr Mortimer because Dr Mortimer did not believe the stories about a supernatural hound.	☐	☒
b. *The Hound of the Baskervilles* shows how a criminal used an old story about a supernatural hound to commit his crime.	☒	☐
c. Conan Doyle became interested in Spiritualism after the death of his son.	☐	☒
d. Spiritualism can be considered a modern scientific religion because it says that we can talk with the dead.	☐	☒
e. Conan Doyle became very angry when people made fun of his belief in fairies.	☐	☒
f. Conan Doyle thought that if people believed in fairies, then they would accept Spiritualism.	☒	☐

Before you read

1 Fill in the gaps with the words below.

this	at	in	because	to	it
for	that	when	together	very	

Sir Henry was 1................ happy to see Sherlock Holmes 2................ we arrived at Baskerville Hall. He told us that he had not gone to dinner at the Stapleton house 3................ of his promise not to leave the Hall.

4................ was a sad moment for me when I told Mr and Mrs Barrymore that Selden was dead. Mrs Barrymore cried bitterly when she heard about her brother.

We ate 5................ in the dining room. Holmes looked 6................ the family pictures with great interest. He pointed at one picture and asked Sir Henry,

'Who is 7................ ?'

'That,' replied Sir Henry, 'is Sir Hugo — the Baskerville who started all 8................ trouble. He was the first Baskerville who saw the hound.'

Holmes studied the picture 9................ a few moments but he made no more comments about Sir Hugo.

Sir Henry went 10................ his room after dinner but Holmes and I remained 11................ the dining room together.

9 **Now listen to the beginning of Chapter Eight to check your answers.**

CHAPTER **EIGHT**

Holmes Gives Sir Henry his Orders

Sir Henry was very happy to see Sherlock Holmes when we arrived at Baskerville Hall. He told us that he had not gone to dinner at the Stapleton house because of his promise not to leave the Hall.

It was a sad moment for me when I told Mr and Mrs Barrymore that Selden was dead. Mrs Barrymore cried bitterly [1] when she heard about her brother.

We ate together in the dining room. Holmes looked at the family pictures with great interest. He pointed at one picture and asked Sir Henry,

'Who is that?'

1. **bitterly** : with emotion.

'That,' replied Sir Henry, 'is Sir Hugo — the Baskerville who started all this trouble. He was the first Baskerville who saw the hound.'

Holmes studied the picture for a few moments but he made no more comments about Sir Hugo.

Sir Henry went to his room after dinner but Holmes and I remained in the dining room together. He went up to the picture of Sir Hugo and looked at it again.

'Who does this man look like?' he asked me.

'Stapleton!' I cried in astonishment. 'The faces are similar. I never thought of it before.'

'There's no doubt that Stapleton is a Baskerville,' Holmes said. 'And he's got Sir Hugo's wicked[1] character as well. I think we're going to find out that Baskerville Hall goes to Mr Stapleton if Sir Henry dies!'

The next morning Holmes told Sir Henry that we had to return to London immediately. Sir Henry did not want us to go, but he agreed in the end.

Holmes gave Sir Henry some instructions. He told him to go to the dinner at the Stapleton house. He told him to go alone, and he told him to explain that we were in London.

'Finally,' Holmes told him, 'I want you to drive to the Stapleton house. When you arrive, send the carriage back here to the Hall. Tell the Stapletons that you're going to walk home over the moor.'

'The moor?' Sir Henry repeated doubtfully. 'But you always told me never to go near there, Mr Holmes!'

'You will be safe tomorrow night, I promise you,' Holmes told him. 'Walk home, but take the path that goes between the

1. **wicked** : bad, evil.

Stapleton house and the Grimpen road. You must not take another path. Is that clear?'

'Very well,' agreed Sir Henry. 'I'll do as you say, Mr Holmes.'

Holmes and I then went to the railway station. There was a boy at the station.

'Have you got any orders, Sir?' he asked Sherlock Holmes.

'Go to London,' Holmes instructed him. 'When you arrive, send Sir Henry a telegram from me. Ask him to send me a book I left behind at Baskerville Hall. Tell him to send it to Baker Street.'

Now I understood part of Holmes's plan. He wanted Sir Henry to tell the Stapletons about his telegram. They would believe that we were both in London.

Now we left the station and went to see Laura Lyons.

'Dr Watson and I think that someone murdered Sir Charles,' Holmes told Mrs Lyons. 'The two suspects are Mr and Mrs Stapleton.'

'Mrs Stapleton!' cried Mrs Lyons in astonishment. 'There is no Mrs Stapleton, Mr Holmes — Mr Stapleton hasn't got a wife!'

'I have all the evidence here,' Holmes announced quietly. He took some documents out of his pocket and showed them to Mrs Lyons. She looked at them unhappily and then she gave them back to Holmes. It was obvious that she believed my friend.

'I thought he loved me,' she said sadly. 'He didn't tell me the truth. I thought he wanted to marry me. You can ask me anything you want, Mr Holmes. I'll tell you the truth.'

'Thank you, Mrs Lyons,' Holmes replied. 'This is what I think happened. Please tell me if I'm right. Mr Stapleton asked you to write the letter to Sir Charles asking to meet him. Then he persuaded you not to go to the meeting that evening. Is that right?'

'Yes,' Mrs Lyons said. 'Stapleton told me not to meet Sir Charles. He said he would find the money for my divorce himself because he loved me. Then I heard that Sir Charles was dead. Stapleton told me to keep silent. He said that he did not want me to be a suspect. He made me feel frightened.'

'Did you think he had secrets?' Holmes asked her.

'Yes, I did,' Mrs Lyons replied. 'I will not keep his secrets from you now, Mr Holmes. I'll tell you everything.'

'You're a danger to Stapleton,' Holmes told her. 'You're lucky to be alive. But you're safe now, I think. We'll talk again.'

Go back to the text

PET 1 **For each question, mark the letter next to the correct answer – A, B, C or D.**

1 Sir Henry had stayed at Baskerville Hall that night because

- **A** ☐ he was afraid of the hound.
- **B** ☐ he did not trust Stapleton.
- **C** ☒ he had promised Watson that he would not go out on the moors alone.
- **D** ☐ he had promised Watson that he would not eat dinner with Stapleton.

2 Holmes understood that Stapleton was a Baskerville because

- **A** ☐ he looked like Sir Henry.
- **B** ☒ he looked like Sir Hugo.
- **C** ☐ he wanted to kill Sir Henry.
- **D** ☐ he had a hound similar to the one that killed Sir Hugo.

3 Holmes surprised Sir Henry when

- **A** ☐ he told him to eat dinner at the Stapleton house.
- **B** ☐ he told him to take a carriage to the Stapleton house.
- **C** ☒ he told him to walk home from the Stapleton house.
- **D** ☐ he asked him about one of the family pictures.

4 Holmes told the boy to go to London and send a telegram to Sir Henry because

- **A** ☐ he wanted to convince Watson that he was in London.
- **B** ☐ he needed the book to complete his investigations.
- **C** ☒ he wanted to convince Stapleton that he was really in London.
- **D** ☐ he wanted to know where Sir Henry was.

5 Which of the following best summarises this chapter?

- **A** ☐ Now we know why Stapleton wants to kill Sir Henry and soon we will have some evidence against him.
- **B** ☒ Now we finally know for certain who the murderer is and soon we will have some evidence against him.
- **C** ☐ We finally know who the murderer is, and tonight we will know why he wants to kill Sir Henry.
- **D** ☐ Now we know who the murderer is, and tonight we will know if there is really a huge hound.

PET **2** **Pretend that you are Laura Lyons. Now that you know the whole truth about Stapleton, you feel very bad about your role in Sir Charles's death. You decide to write Sir Henry a letter to explain to him exactly what happened. In your letter of about 100 words tell him about:**

- your marriage and your relationship with your father
- what Stapleton promised you
- why you never went to the meeting with Sir Charles
- why you never told the police about what happened

You can begin like this:

Dear Sir Henry,

Of course I was extremely sad about Sir Charles's death. Now, however, that I realise that I myself played a role in his tragic death I feel even worse. Please believe me though when I tell you that I knew nothing of Mr Stapleton's wicked plan.

First let me explain that..

Yours sincerely,

Laura Lyons

'Sir Hugo was the first Baskerville who saw the hound'

Look at the following sentences:

- *Sir Hugo was the first Baskerville who saw the hound.*
- *This is a page of the letter which Laura Lyons sent to Sir Charles.*
- *That is the gate which opens onto the moors.*
- *This is the hut where Sherlock Holmes stayed.*
- *Laura Lyons is the woman that sent Sir Charles a letter.*
- *Here is the telegram that I sent to Barrymore.*

The underlined part of the sentence is called a **defining relative clause.**

A defining relative clause is essential to the meaning of the sentence: it tells us what person, place or thing we are talking about.

A defining relative clause is not separated from the rest of the sentence by a comma.

Notice that:
- 'which' is only used for things
- 'who' is only used for people
- 'that' can be used for both people and things
- 'where' is used to talk about places

3 Fill in the gaps with *where, which* or *who*.

a. This is the house ....where.... Mr Sherlock Holmes lives.
b. Devonshire is the part of England ....where.... *The Hound of the Baskervilles* takes place.
c. *A Study in Scarlet* was the book ....which.... introduced Sherlock Holmes to the world.
d. Edgar Allan Poe is the writer ....who.... invented the modern detective story.
e. There is the pipe ....which.... Sherlock Holmes smokes when he is thinking about a difficult case.
f. Edinburgh is the city ....where.... Sir Arthur Conan Doyle was born.
g. Harriet is my friend ....who.... always brings good things to eat.

4 Identify the following characters using sentences with defining relative clauses.

a. She wrote Sir Charles a letter.
Laura Lyons was the woman who wrote Sir Charles a letter.
b. She helped her brother by bringing him food.
c. He wrote a warning to his sons in 1742.
d. He loved arguing and looking at the moors through his telescope.
e. He will inherit Baskerville Hall if Sir Henry dies.
f. She pretended to be her husband's sister.
g. He died because he was wearing another man's clothing.

INTERNET PROJECT

Connect to the Internet and go to www.blackcat.vicensvives.net. Insert the title or part of the title of the book into our search engine (*buscador*). Click on *The Hound of the Baskervilles*. Click on *Project links*, and then on the relevant link for this project.

Arthur Conan Doyle decided to write *The Hound of the Baskervilles* after a long stay on the Devonshire moors. When he was there he heard legends about a hound from hell, and he also visited the famous Dartmoor Prison (where Selden was a prisoner).

Using one of the major search engines or your teacher's suggestions find out about the Dartmoor National Park:

- Where it is located
- What remains of prehistoric man can be found there
- What animals live there

Download some photos of the park and show the class your favourites.

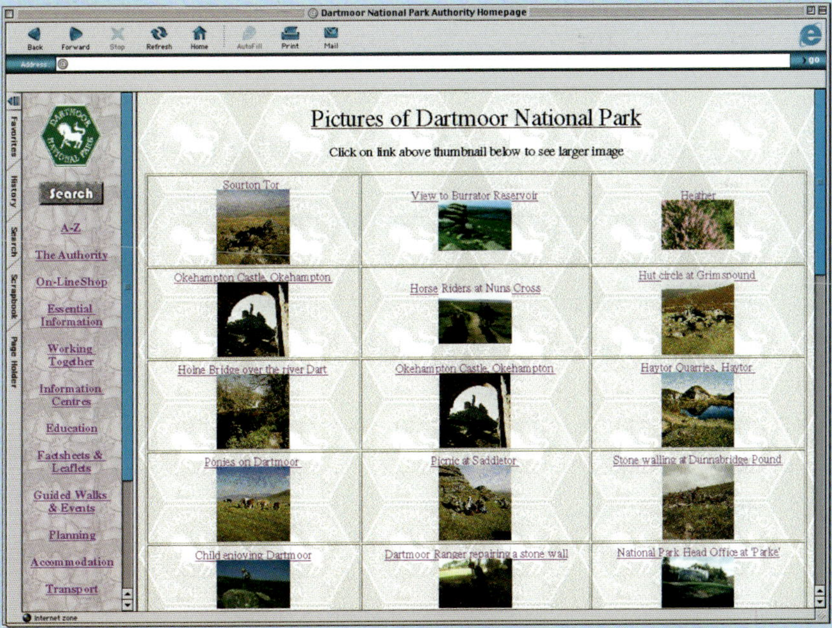

Before you read

PET **1** **Listen to the beginning of Chapter Nine. For each question, put a tick (✓) in the correct box.**

10

1 What did Holmes and Watson carry with them when they went to Stapleton's house?

A ☐ rifles
B ☐ revolvers
C ☐ knives

2 What did Watson see when he looked through the window of Stapleton's house?

A ☐ Stapleton and Sir Henry
B ☐ Stapleton, his wife and Sir Henry
C ☐ just Stapleton

3 What did Stapleton do when he came out of the house?

A ☐ He went to a hut and opened its door.
B ☐ He went out onto the moors with a huge hound.
C ☐ He went out onto the moors by himself.

4 What was especially frightening about the hound?

A ☐ It was completely black.
B ☐ It made an incredibly strange noise when it ran.
C ☐ Its head seemed to be on fire.

5 Who finally killed the hound?

A ☐ Holmes
B ☐ Watson
C ☐ Sir Henry

CHAPTER **NINE**

The Appearance of the Hound of the Baskervilles

Holmes and I went to the Stapleton house when it was dark. We carried our revolvers with us and we walked very quietly.

'Look through the windows,' Holmes ordered me. 'I want to know where Mr Stapleton and Sir Henry are.'

I could see Mr Stapleton and Sir Henry sitting together, but I could not see Mrs Stapleton.

Then Stapleton came out of the house for a moment. He went towards a little hut in the garden. He opened the door of the hut and I could hear a strange noise inside it. Then Stapleton went back inside the house.

Now the fog began to come down. It was very heavy and we could not see very far in front of us.

'We must be very careful,' Holmes warned me. 'We don't want to lose Sir Henry in the fog.'

Now we heard someone leave the house. It was Sir Henry. He walked along the path as Holmes had told him to do. Sir Henry seemed nervous, and he kept looking behind him.

'It's coming!' Holmes whispered excitedly. He pointed just behind Sir Henry. I looked into the darkness. I wanted to see what this monster was.

There was an enormous hound following Sir Henry. It was the biggest dog I had ever seen. But the really frightening thing about it was its eyes. They shone in the darkness, and flames came out of its mouth. Its whole head seemed to be on fire!

The hound ran after Sir Henry. Sir Henry knew it was there now, and he was afraid. He began to run away from it as fast as he could. The hound ran after him.

Holmes and I fired our revolvers at the monster but it did not stop. It continued to run after Sir Henry. The hound jumped onto the poor man and seized[1] his throat. Sir Henry fell to the ground.

Holmes ran towards them. Holmes fired his gun before the animal could attack the man on the ground. END

Sir Henry was unconscious. He was not injured[2] but he was terrified. At last he opened his eyes and looked at my friend.

'What was it?' he asked. He looked at the body of the hound in fear.

1. **seized** : took hold of violently.
2. **injured** : hurt.

Holmes stepped forward and examined the body of the animal. Its head still burnt with a strange light.

'Phosphorous paint,' he told us. 'Someone put this on the hound to make it even more terrible. But it's dead now. You're safe now, Sir Henry.'

'You saved my life, Sir,' Sir Henry told Holmes.

'Now you must stay here for a while, Sir Henry,' Holmes ordered him. 'Watson and I are going back to the Stapleton house. I want to catch that man!'

Holmes and I walked back to the Stapleton house through the fog.

'I don't think Stapleton will be there any more,' my friend told me. 'But we must search the house. I'm sure he heard our revolvers. He knows Sir Henry is still alive.'

The door of the house was open and we went inside. The rooms of the house downstairs were empty and we climbed the stairs. The rooms here were empty as well, but there was one room that we could not open.

'He's in here,' I said. 'I heard a noise inside this room.'

Holmes and I broke the door open and went inside. Inside the room we saw a figure covered in a white sheet and tied up. It was Mrs Stapleton. We freed her. There were a lot of marks on her body.

'He beat her,' Holmes said angrily. We put her into a chair. After a few minutes she was able to speak.

'Is he safe?' she asked us. 'Did he run away?'

'Mr Stapleton will not escape us,' Holmes told her sternly.

'I'm not talking about my husband,' Mrs Stapleton said, 'I'm talking about Sir Henry. Is Sir Henry safe?'

'Sir Henry is safe and the hound is dead,' I told her.

'I'm glad,' Mrs Stapleton said. 'My husband is a very cruel man. Look what he did to me!'

She showed us the marks on her hands and arms.

'Where is he?' Holmes asked her.

'There's an old house in the middle of the moor,' she explained. 'That's where he kept the hound. I'm sure you'll find him there.'

'We can't go into the Grimpen marsh tonight with all this fog,' Holmes decided.

We went back to Sir Henry and carried him to Baskerville Hall. He was very sad when he understood that the girl he loved was really Stapleton's wife. He became ill and we sent for the local doctor.

The next morning there was no fog and Mrs Stapleton took us into the Grimpen Marsh. We found the little house but it was empty. All we found there were some old bones: Stapleton had used them to feed the hound. We searched the moor all day but we couldn't find Mr Stapleton anywhere. All we saw was an old boot that had belonged to Sir Henry. Stapleton had taken it from the hotel in London and used it to set the hound after Sir Henry.

'Stapleton lost his way in the fog,' Holmes decided. 'He is dead, Watson. He sank in the marsh. I'm sure of it.'

Go back to the text

1 Answer the following questions.

phosphorous paint

a. What made the hound look as though it were on fire?

b. Who is Mrs Stapleton referring to when she says, 'Is he safe?'? To Henry

c. Where did Stapleton escape to? old house

d. What did Holmes and Watson find out on the moor? bones to feed the Hound

e. What happened to Stapleton in the end?

He sank in the marsh

'He was not injured'

Look at these active sentences and their equivalent in the **passive**.

- *The hound did not injure him — He* ***was not injured by*** *the hound.*
- *The postman delivers the post every day — The post* ***is delivered*** *every day.*
- *The police arrested the criminal — The criminal* ***was arrested.***

We form the passive of the Present and Past Simple with the correct form of the verb *to be* (am, are, is — was, were) and the past participle.

Generally we use the passive when:

- we consider the action more important than the agent (the person or thing that does the action):

  This book was printed in 1989.

  This bridge was constructed in 2001.

- the agent is obvious or already known:

  The murderer was arrested.

  Sir Henry was not injured. (It is clear within the context of the story that it was not the hound that injured Sir Henry.)

- the subject of the active sentence is 'they' or 'people':

  French is spoken in Quebec.

  The euro is used in Germany.

- the agent of the action is not known:

  Sir Christian was murdered (the police do not know who the murderer is).

  My car was stolen last night.

When we want to say who the agent is we use 'by':

Sir Henry's old boot was taken by Stapleton.

The daughter of the farmer was kidnapped by Sir Hugo.

Sometimes, even if we wish to emphasise the action, it is necessary to mention the agent:

Parades are adored by New Yorkers.

Mr Barrymore told us that the letter was written by Laura Lyons.

2 Change the following sentences to the passive. Say who the agent is where necessary.

a. The waiter did not bring our dinner until ten o'clock.

Our dinner wasn't brought until ten o'clock

b. The English sing the song 'Auld Lang Syne' on New Year's Eve.

On New Years eve the song "Auld Lang Syne" is song by the English

c. Somebody left the gate open last night.

Last night somebody left the gate open

d. They produce a lot of good wine in California.

In Califorma a lot of good wine is produce

e. The American writer Edgar Allan Poe created the first scientific detective.

The First scientific detecti was created by the american writer Edgar Allan Poe

f. People saw a huge hound out on the moors.

On the moors a huge hound was saw

g. A big black cat bit me.

I was bit by a big black cat

h. The snow totally covered my car.

My car was totally covered with snow

Before you read

1 Listen to the beginning of Chapter Ten and fill in the gaps.

(**1**) .... and I returned to London. I still did not (**2**) .... all the facts of the case, and I asked my friend to explain everything to me.

'I have spoken to (**3**) .... and she has explained things to me.' Holmes told me.

'We know from the family pictures that Stapleton was a member of the (**4**) .... family. He was the son of Rodger Baskerville the criminal. Rodger Baskerville died in (**5**) .... but he had a son, also called Rodger — the man we knew as (**6**) .... He married a beautiful young woman named Beryl Garcia. The couple came to England and pretended to be (**7**) .... and (**8**) .... instead of husband and wife.

'Stapleton knew that all the Baskerville property was his if (**9**) .... and Sir Henry died — and he decided to kill them.

'He heard the story of the Hound of the Baskervilles, and he knew that Sir Charles believed in the old stories. Stapleton decided to buy a (**10**) .... and hide it on the (**11**) ....

'It was (**12**) .... to kill Sir Charles because he had a weak heart. He asked Laura Lyons to write the letter to Sir Charles to meet him in the garden one (**13**) .... At the last minute he persuaded her not to go there. Stapleton wanted Sir Charles to be alone so that he could (**14**) .... him to death with the hound.

'The rest was easy. When Sir Charles saw the hound with the phosphorous (**15**) .... on his face he died of fright.

Now read the text to check your answers.

CHAPTER **TEN**

Holmes Explains the Case

Holmes and I returned to London. I still did not understand all the facts of the case, and I asked my friend to explain everything to me.

'I have spoken to Mrs Stapleton and she has explained things to me.' Holmes told me.

'We know from the family pictures that Stapleton was a member of the Baskerville family. He was the son of Rodger Baskerville the criminal. Rodger Baskerville died in South America but he had a son, also called Rodger — the man we knew as Stapleton. He married a beautiful young woman named Beryl Garcia. The couple came to England and pretended to be brother and sister instead of husband and wife.

'Stapleton knew that all the Baskerville property was his if Sir Charles and Sir Henry died — and he decided to kill them.

'He heard the story of the Hound of the Baskervilles, and he knew that Sir Charles believed in the old stories. Stapleton decided to buy a hound and hide it on the moors.

'It was easy to kill Sir Charles because he had a weak heart. He asked Laura Lyons to write the letter to Sir Charles to meet him in the garden one evening. At the last minute he persuaded her not to go there. Stapleton wanted Sir Charles to be alone so that he could frighten him to death with the hound.

'The rest was easy. When Sir Charles saw the hound with the phosphorous paint on his face he died of fright.

'Then Stapleton came to London to follow Sir Henry and kill him there. He wanted one of Sir Henry's shoes to give to the hound. He knew the hound would follow the scent of Sir Henry's shoe. First of all he took a new one, but it didn't work as there was no scent. So he had to steal an old shoe. When he realised that I was helping Sir Henry, Stapleton decided to return to the moors.

'Everything began to go wrong for Stapleton when his wife refused to help him any more with his wicked plans to destroy the Baskervilles. That is why he beat her and left her in the house. Her love for him slowly turned to hatred as she understood the kind of man he really was.'

Holmes smiled at me.

'And now, Watson, I think there will be just time for us to go to the theatre tonight — our case is closed.'

Go back to the text

PET **1** **Decide if each statement is correct or incorrect. If it is correct, mark A. If it is not correct, mark B.**

		A	B
1	Stapleton was the son of Roger Baskerville.	☐	☐
2	Stapleton wanted to kill Sir Henry to get the Baskerville property.	☐	☐
3	Stapleton bought a hound because he knew that Sir Henry believed in the legend of the Hound of the Baskervilles.	☐	☐
4	Laura Lyons did not go to see Sir Charles because she realised that Stapleton was an evil man.	☐	☐
5	Stapleton wanted the hound to attack and kill Sir Charles.	☐	☐
6	Stapleton decided not to try and kill Sir Henry in London because he saw Sherlock Holmes with him there.	☐	☐
7	Stapleton's wife began to hate him when she realised that he was in love with Laura Lyons.	☐	☐

Now correct the incorrect statements.

T: GRADE 6

2 **Topic – Fashion**

Look again at the pictures in the book. Prepare a talk for your class about fashion. Use the questions below to help you.

- What do the men wear when they are walking about on the moors?
- What do people wear nowadays when they do outdoor activities like trekking in the moors or in the mountains?
- What do the young women in the book wear?
- What might young women today wear in similar circumstances?

3 **Number the paragraphs (a-i) of this summary of Chapters Six to Ten in the correct order. Then fill in the gaps with the words in the box.**

cliff	escaped	advice	path	enormous	next	sad
tied	fired	divorce	pictures	huts	property	lovely
roof	wife	fog	fault	shone	fall	evidence

a. ☐ They then returned to Baskerville Hall and told Mrs Barrymore the .... news. That night at dinner Holmes asked Sir Henry about one of the family .... Sir Henry told him that it was of Sir Hugo. After Sir Henry went to his room, Holmes told Watson that Stapleton looked incredibly similar to Sir Hugo, and that he was certain that Stapleton was a Baskerville. This meant that if Sir Henry died, the Baskerville .... went to Stapleton.

b. [1] After Barrymore told Watson about the letter, he decided to pay a visit to Mrs Laura Lyons. He told her that he knew she had written a letter to Sir Charles. At first she became angry, but then she admitted that she had wanted to ask Sir Charles for some .... She wanted to .... her husband.

c. ☐ After this Watson decided to discover who the mysterious stranger on the moors was. As he was walking towards the moors Mr Frankland called to him and invited him up on his .... Frankland told him that he watched a boy bringing food to the escaped murderer. Just then, the boy appeared and Watson saw him disappear over a hill.

d. ☐ Watson and Holmes then went into the house where they found Mrs Stapleton .... up. They freed her, and she told them everything about her husband. The next day, after the fog had lifted, they walked out on the moors to an old house where Stapleton had kept the hound. They did not, however, find Stapleton. Stapleton, it seems, had lost his way on the moors and drowned.

e. ☐ As they were talking, they heard the sound of a hound. They ran towards it and arrived at the edge of a .... Below they saw the body of a man who appeared to be Sir Henry. Holmes was extremely sad because he felt that Sir Henry's death was his

.... However, when he went down to examine the body more closely he saw that the dead man was actually Selden.

f. ☐ He began to walk along the .... Then they saw an .... dog running after Sir Henry. Its eyes .... and a flame came out of its mouth. Sir Henry began to run and the hound followed him. Holmes and Watson both .... their revolvers but the hound did not stop. It jumped on Sir Henry. Fortunately, though, Holmes ran up and shot the hound dead.

g. ☐ Watson then walked towards the hill. He saw a series of .... and went into one where he found some pots and pans. The mysterious stranger had been living there. Suddenly Watson heard somebody outside say, 'What a .... evening, Watson.' The mysterious stranger was none other than Sherlock Holmes. Holmes told Watson everything that he had discovered. He told him that Miss Stapleton was really Mr Stapleton's ...., and that he had wanted Sir Henry to .... in love with her so that he could get close to Sir Henry.

h. ☐ Just then Stapleton appeared. He asked what happened. Holmes and Watson said that the dead man was Selden, the .... murderer. Selden then asked Holmes if the Hound of Baskervilles was involved. Holmes said that it was not, and that he was not interested in legends. In fact, he said, he was going back to London. When Selden left, Holmes told Watson that he had a plan to catch Selden because they still had no .... against him.

i. ☐ The .... morning Holmes told Sir Henry that he was returning to London. He also told Sir Henry to go to Stapleton's for dinner alone. Sir Henry had to drive there in a carriage, and then walk home across the moors. That night Holmes and Watson went to Stapleton's house and waited. They saw Stapleton come out and open the door of a hut. Then he went inside the house. Then the .... came down and it became extremely difficult to see. After a while they heard Sir Henry leave the house.

PET **1** **Read the questions about *The Hound of the Baskervilles* below. For each question, mark the letter next to the correct answer — A, B, C or D.**

1 When Holmes first hears the story of Sir Hugo and the huge hound he thinks that it
- **A** ☐ shows that God punishes the wicked and forgives the innocent.
- **B** ☐ is a true story.
- **C** ☐ shows how Sir Charles died.
- **D** ☒ is a good story for frightening children.

2 The newspaper article says that Sir Charles died because
- **A** ☒ he had a weak heart.
- **B** ☐ he was attacked by a huge hound.
- **C** ☐ he was killed by Stapleton.
- **D** ☐ he was punished for his wicked actions.

3 Sir Charles seemed to walk down the Alley on his toes because
- **A** ☐ the rain had changed the appearance of his footprints.
- **B** ☐ it was not possible to leave good footprints on the path.
- **C** ☒ he had run away from something.
- **D** ☐ his shoes left strange footprints that looked like toe-prints.

4 Stapleton took Sir Henry's shoes because
- **A** ☐ he wanted to frighten Sir Henry.
- **B** ☐ he wanted to confuse Sherlock Holmes.
- **C** ☒ he needed something with Sir Henry's scent for the hound.
- **D** ☐ he thought they belonged to Sir Charles.

5 Who was the man with a black beard that followed Sir Henry in London?
- **A** ☒ Stapleton.
- **B** ☒ Barrymore.
- **C** ☐ Sherlock Holmes.
- **D** ☐ Mr Frankland.

6 When Watson and Sir Henry arrived on the moors they saw a soldier who was looking for
- **A** ☒ an escaped prisoner.
- **B** ☐ Sir Charles's murderer.
- **C** ☐ the man with the black beard.
- **D** ☐ the Hound of the Baskervilles.

7 Watson knew that Barrymore was lying about his wife when he said that she had not been crying during the night because

A ☐ Barrymore looked frightened when Watson asked him about his wife.
B ☒ he saw that Mrs Barrymore's eyes were red and she looked sad.
C ☐ she was the only woman in the house.
D ☐ Watson saw her crying the next morning.

8 Horses often died on the moors because

A ☒ they drowned in the marsh.
B ☐ they were killed by the hound.
C ☐ they could not find enough food.
D ☐ they were killed by sheep dogs.

9 When Miss Stapleton first met Watson she told him to go back to London because

A ☐ she didn't want him to discover Mr Stapleton's plans.
B ☒ she was afraid that Mr Stapleton wanted to hurt him.
C ☒ she thought he was Sir Henry and she knew Mr Stapleton planned to kill him.
D ☐ she thought he was Sir Henry and she did not want him to fall in love with her.

10 Mr Barrymore went to the window with a candle to

A ☐ check if the window was closed.
B ☒ signal to the escaped prisoner.
C ☐ signal to the boy who was working for Holmes.
D ☐ signal to Stapleton.

11 Who was the mysterious stranger that Watson saw on the moors?

A ☒ Sherlock Holmes.
B ☐ Mr Barrymore.
C ☐ Mr Frankland.
D ☐ Mr Stapleton

12 Laura Lyons wanted to talk to Sir Charles to

A ☐ ask his advice about her father.
B ☒ ask him to protect her.
C ☐ ask his advice about getting married.
D ☒ ask his advice about getting divorced.

13 The hound ran after Selden because
- A ☐ Selden was alone on the moors.
- B ☐ Selden had the scent of food on his clothing.
- C ☒ Selden was wearing Sir Henry's old clothing and so had Sir Henry's scent.
- D ☐ Selden looked like Sir Henry because he was wearing his clothes.

14 Holmes was very interested in the painting of Sir Hugo because
- A ☐ Sir Hugo was the first Baskerville to see the hound.
- B ☐ Sir Hugo looked like a criminal.
- C ☒ Stapleton looked just like Sir Hugo.
- D ☐ Sir Henry looked just like Sir Hugo.

15 Laura Lyons did not tell anybody that she was going to meet Sir Charles on the night of his death because
- A ☐ she was afraid of Mr Stapleton.
- B ☐ Mr Stapleton said that he wanted to get her the money for her divorce.
- C ☒ she was afraid of becoming a suspect.
- D ☐ she did not think it was important.

16 Holmes told the boy to send Sir Henry a telegram from London because
- A ☐ he wanted Sir Henry to send him a book he had left at Baskerville Hall.
- B ☒ he wanted to convince both Sir Henry and Stapleton that he was in London.
- C ☐ he wanted to convince Sir Henry and Watson that he was in London.
- D ☐ he wanted to see if Sir Henry was really at Baskerville Hall and not in London.

17 When Holmes and Watson went into Stapleton's house they found
- A ☒ Mrs Stapleton wrapped in a sheet and tied up.
- B ☐ Mrs Laura Lyons wrapped in a sheet and tied up.
- C ☐ some old bones that Stapleton had used to feed the hound.
- D ☐ Sir Henry's old shoe.

18 Stapleton beat his wife and tied her up because

- A [ ] she had fallen in love with Sir Henry.
- B [x] she refused to help him anymore in his plans to kill Sir Henry.
- C [ ] he wanted to marry Laura Lyons.
- D [ ] he wanted to have all the Baskerville property for himself.

2 For the following questions choose from the characters (A-K).

A. Sherlock Holmes
B. Dr Watson
C. Sir Charles Baskerville
D. Sir Henry Baskerville
E. Mr Stapleton
F. Miss Stapleton
G. Laura Lyons
H. Mrs Barrymore
I. Mr Barrymore
J. Selden
k. Dr Mortimer

1. [I] Who found Sir Charles's body?
2. [I] Who lied to protect his wife?
3. [A] Who killed the Hound of the Baskervilles?
4. [E] Whose father was a criminal?
5. [H] Who told Watson that Selden was really Mrs Barrymore's brother?
6. [A] Who discovered that Mr Stapleton was married?
7. [D] Who was in love with Miss Stapleton?
8. [J] Who died by falling over a cliff?
9. [C] Who died of fright?
10. [C] Who told Dr Mortimer about the Hound of the Baskervilles?
11. [I] Who told Sir Henry that Sir Charles went to meet a woman on the night of his death?
12. [H] Who tried to protect his/her brother?
13. [E] Whose hobby was collecting insects?
14. [A] Who told Watson that he was in London when he was really on the moors?
15. [F] Who sent Sir Henry a letter telling him not to go to the moor because it was dangerous?
16. [K] Who was embarrassed because he believed that the Hound of the Baskervilles actually existed?